Irregular Migrants

A new era of international migration has been accompanied by increasingly restrictive immigration controls to manage migration to more developed countries. The consequence has been fewer routes to enter and/or stay in countries in a regularised way and as a result, an increase in the numbers of undocumented migrants. In this situation undocumented migrants, especially in relation to immigration controls and internal security have come to occupy an important role on the policy agenda of many nation states. The control and regulation of undocumented migrants has become an increasingly politicised issue. This edited collection brings together cutting edge scholarly research papers to explore undocumented migration at the international, national and individual levels. Starting with an overview of the literature on undocumented migration this book explores some of the key areas of research and policy in this area. This includes the making of undocumented migrants, the journey and processes, experiences of being undocumented at the individual level, collective action and return. This fascinating book explores the many facets of undocumented migration and of being an undocumented migrant in different geographical contexts that include Europe, Southern Africa, Central America and North America.

This book was originally published as a special issue of *Ethnic and Racial Studies.*

Alice Bloch is Professor of Sociology at City University London, UK. She is also co-editor of *Race and Ethnicity in the 21st Century* (2010).

Milena Chimienti is Lecturer in Sociology at City University London, UK. She is also author of *Prostitution et Migration: La dynamique de l'agir faible* (2009).

Ethnic and Racial Studies

Series editors: Martin Bulmer, *University of Surrey, UK*, and John Solomos, *City University London, UK*

The journal *Ethnic and Racial Studies* was founded in 1978 by John Stone to provide an international forum for high quality research on race, ethnicity, nationalism and ethnic conflict. At the time the study of race and ethnicity was still a relatively marginal sub-field of sociology, anthropology and political science. In the intervening period the journal has provided a space for the discussion of core theoretical issues, key developments and trends, and for the dissemination of the latest empirical research.

It is now the leading journal in its field and has helped to shape the development of scholarly research agendas. *Ethnic and Racial Studies* attracts submissions from scholars in a diverse range of countries, fields of scholarship and crosses disciplinary boundaries. It has moved from being a quarterly to being published monthly and it is now available in both printed and electronic form.

The Ethnic and Racial Studies book series contains a wide range of the journal's special issues. These special issues are an important contribution to the work of the journal, where leading social science academics bring together articles on specific themes and issues that are linked to the broad intellectual concerns of *Ethnic and Racial Studies.* The series editors work closely with the guest editors of the special issues to ensure that they meet the highest quality standards possible. Through publishing these special issues as a series of books, we hope to allow a wider audience of both scholars and students from across the social sciences to engage with the work of *Ethnic and Racial Studies.*

Other titles in the series include:

The Transnational Political Participation of Immigrants
Edited by Jean-Michel Lafleur and Marco Martiniello

New Racial Missions of Policing: International Perspectives on Evolving Law-Enforcement Politics
Edited by Paul Amar

Anthropology of Migration and Multiculturalism
Edited by Steven Vertovec

Migrant Politics and Mobilisation: Exclusion, Engagements, Incorporation
Edited by Davide Però and John Solomos

Retheorizing Race and Whiteness in the 21st Century
Edited by Charles A. Gallagher and France Winddance Twine

Theorising Integration and Assimilation
Edited by Jens Schneider and Maurice Crul

Ethnic and Racial Minorities in Asia: Inclusion or Exclusion?
Edited by Michelle Ann Miller

Diasporas, Cultures and Identities
Edited by Martin Bulmer and John Solomos

Gender, Race and Religion: Intersections and Challenges
Edited by Martin Bulmer and John Solomos

Latino Identity in Contemporary America
Edited by Martin Bulmer and John Solomos

Migration: Policies, Practices, Activism
Edited by Martin Bulmer and John Solomos

Nationalism and National Identities
Edited by Martin Bulmer and John Solomos

Young People, Ethnicity and Social Capital
Edited by Tracey Reynolds

Cosmopolitan Sociability
Edited by Tsypylma Darieva, Nina Glick Schiller and Sandra Gruner-Domic

Methods and Contexts in the Study of Muslim Minorities: Visible and Invisible Muslims
Edited by Nadia Jeldtoft and Jørgen S. Nielsen

Irregular Migrants: Policy, Politics, Motives and Everyday Lives
Edited by Alice Bloch and Milena Chimienti

Fighting Discrimination in Europe: The Case for a Race-Conscious Approach
Edited by Mathias Möschel, Costanza Hermanin and Michele Grigolo

Responses to Stigmatization in Comparative Perspective
Edited by Michele Lamont and Nissim Mizrachi

Health Care and Immigration: Understanding the Connections
Edited by Patricia Fernandez-Kelly and Alejandro Portes

Gender, Migration and the Media
Edited by Myria Georgiou

Accounting for Ethnic and Racial Diversity: The Challenge of Enumeration
Edited by Patrick Simon and Victor Piché

Irregular Migrants

Policy, Politics, Motives and Everyday Lives

Edited by

Alice Bloch and Milena Chimienti

Routledge
Taylor & Francis Group
LONDON AND NEW YORK

ETHNIC AND RACIAL STUDIES

First published 2012
by Routledge
2 Park Square, Milton Park, Abingdon, Oxon, OX14 4RN

Simultaneously published in the USA and Canada
by Routledge
605 Third Avenue, New York, NY 10017

Routledge is an imprint of the Taylor & Francis Group, an informa business

This book is a reproduction of *Ethnic and Racial Studies*, volume 34, issue 8. The Publisher requests to those authors who may be citing this book to state, also, the bibliographical details of the special issue on which the book was based.

British Library Cataloguing in Publication Data
A catalogue record for this book is available from the British Library

ISBN13: 978-0-415-50413-3 (hbk)

Typeset in Times New Roman
by Taylor & Francis Books

Publisher's Note
The publisher would like to make readers aware that the chapters in this book may be referred to as articles as they are identical to the articles published in the special issue. The publisher accepts responsibility for any inconsistencies that may have arisen in the course of preparing this volume for print.

Contents

Notes on contributors

Alice Bloch is Professor in the Department of Sociology at City University London, UK.

Brianna Castro received her BA in Public Policy at the University of North Carolina, USA in 2009.

Sergio Chávez is an Assistant Professor in the Department of Sociology at Rice University, USA.

Milena Chimienti is Lecturer in the Department of Sociology at City University London, UK.

Jacqueline Maria Hagan is Professor in the Department of Sociology at the University of North Carolina, at Chapel Hill, USA.

Barbara Laubenthal is a Lecturer in the Faculty of Social Sciences at the Ruhr-Universität Bochum, Germany.

Nestor Rodriguez is Professor in the Department of Sociology at the University of Texas at Austin, USA.

Blair Rutherford is Professor in the Department of Sociology and Anthropology at Carleton University, Canada.

Liza Schuster is Reader in Sociology in the Department of Sociology at City University London, UK.

Nando Sigona is Senior Research Officer at the Refugee Studies Centre and Research Associate at the ESRC Centre on Migration, Policy and Society (COMPAS), both at the University of Oxford, UK.

Roger Zetter is Professor Emeritus in Refugee Studies at the Refugee Studies Centre, University of Oxford, UK.

Irregular migration in a globalizing world

Alice Bloch and Milena Chimienti

Abstract

This introduction to the special issue 'Irregular Migrants: Policy, Politics, Motives and Everyday Lives' outlines the changing patterns of irregular migration at the end of the twentieth century and the start of the twenty-first century, explores the ways in which irregular migration has been analysed conceptually and empirically, highlights the contribution the volume as a whole makes to the literature in this domain and examines the key emergent themes from the papers in this volume. Finally, the paper concludes by suggesting gaps in our knowledge and areas for further research.

Introduction

At the start of the twenty-first century, irregular migration is a global and visible phenomenon. First, it occurs in most countries: it is estimated that in 2004, between 10 and 15 per cent of the world's migrants were living in an irregular situation, which is equivalent to between 20 million and 30 million people (International Organization for Migration/ILO 2004; Koser 2010). Second, irregular migration has become a concern for different state and non-state actors. This includes governments who want to manage migration, human rights activists and campaigning organizations which focus on the lack of rights experienced by irregular migrants, employers who want to maintain access to 'cheap' and 'compliant' labour, travel companies and firms who are concerned by the prospect of sanctions for transporting people with the wrong or no documentation and irregular migrants themselves who try to survive despite their situation of vulnerability. Third, in several countries collective action among irregular migrants, to try and access rights, has made them more visible. This special issue of *Ethnic and Racial Studies* aims to outline the position of irregular migrants globally and to address some of the key conceptual debates about the context and challenges of irregular migration. We use the term 'irregular migration' to refer to people who do not have a residence status in the country in which they are residing.

The special issue has its origins in a workshop held at City University London in September 2009. Paper contributions were invited from scholars working within different social science disciplines and focusing on different geographical contexts. The papers explored, theoretically and empirically, the complex interactions, processes and lived experiences of irregular migration at the international, national and individual levels.

The seven papers in this issue draw on a range of conceptual perspectives and on empirical research carried out in different countries and settings. The papers explore irregular migration in the US (Hagan, Mullis and Rodriguez), Europe (Bloch, Sigona and Zetter; Chimienti; Laubenthal; Schuster), Mexico (Chavez) and South Africa (Rutherford). The combined contributions provide a critical perspective and aim to encourage more reflection on this global issue through regional comparisons and through a multi-level analysis of the relationship between structure and agency in the irregularizing process and in the experiences of irregularity.

The following section will contextualize the special issue by discussing the changing and ongoing patterns of irregular migration. This will be followed by a discussion of the key literature in this area and the core themes of the papers in this volume. The conclusion will highlight gaps in knowledge and areas for further research.

Changing and ongoing patterns of irregular migration

It is surprising how little change there has been in the patterns of irregular migration since the 1970s when Portes (1978) edited a special issue of *International Migration Review*. The causes of irregular migration, its forms and the policies to deal with the phenomena show several similarities over time and place.

Portes argues that the causes of irregular migration are mainly related to 'structural determinants in both sending and receiving countries' (1978, p. 477) and therefore benefit both sending and receiving countries. Migrant-receiving countries need the cheap and flexible labour offered by irregular migrants while sending countries have the tensions created by underemployment, inequality and political, social and economic uncertainty partially alleviated.

Although these economic push-pull factors still have contemporary relevance, there are additional factors that precipitate irregular migration and irregularity. These factors include the children of irregular migrants who are born into irregularity and the partners of irregular migrants, asylum seekers who have had their cases rejected, visa over-stayers (student, holiday and work) as well as those who enter clandestinely. This diversity highlights that irregularity can be a process and/or migration strategy, rather than a defined 'end-state' (Jordan and Düvell 2002; Bloch *et al.* this issue), and is, among other factors, related to the increased difficulty of migrating legally to EU member states.

In a globalized era, demand for both high- and low-skilled migrant workers in northern economies has grown (Castles and Miller 2009). However alongside the need for labour, immigration controls have been developed at nation-state and supra-national levels, creating a disjuncture between economic and political interests regarding immigration, in what Hollifield (1992) calls the 'liberal paradox' of 'open' markets and 'closed' political communities. This intensified attempt to manage migration, including with technological tools, obliges individuals to use different and sometimes fluid immigration statuses and strategies. In other words, legal immigration has become more difficult and is increasingly limited to the privileged few.

At the policy level Portes, focusing on the US case, has noted a number of strategies envisaged by the US to 'solve the problem of irregular migration' (1978, p. 469–70). These strategies included supporting development in sending countries, closing borders, penalizing employers who employ irregular migrants, apprehending migrant smugglers and offering amnesties to irregular migrants. Although irregular migration became an issue in Europe later than in North America because in Europe, before the 1980s, it was a tolerated and accepted consequence of the guest worker schemes, similar interventions have subsequently taken place in Europe.

First, both have implemented policies to repress the flow of irregular migrants. These have included both the 'externalization of border control' and 'interior social control' such as increasing the number of countries of origin that require visas (Trianfadyllidou 2010; Hagan *et al.* in this issue). In the context of the European Union (EU), the control of external borders takes the form of cooperation within the EU zone and between EU member and non-member states. EU member states co-operate in a number of ways, including the operationalization of Dublin I and II regulations (see Schuster in this volume) which enable EU member states to deport asylum seekers to the first country of asylum. The cooperation between EU and non-EU states means that EU members can return a non-national to a safe third country outside the EU.

The second type of policy includes 'delocalization of the border' and 'remote control' which means that control takes place beyond borders

(Guiraudon 2003; Walters 2006). These measures diversify modes of surveillance and in recent years have incorporated travel companies, employers, service providers and private citizens into the arsenal of immigration controls used by the state. This includes transport agencies through liability fines for carriers for transporting people without the correct documentation, employers by fining those caught employing people without the correct documentation as well as NGOs, health providers and educational establishments who are asked to monitor the immigration status of their service users (Coutin 1993; De Genova 2002). This has been formalized at the EU level since the 1990s where directives suggesting a 'minimum level of common standards', concerning for instance sanctions against carriers and employers that have been put in place (Directive 2009/52/EC; see also Triandafyllidou 2010, pp. 35–36).

Border control policies, internal controls and the remote control of borders have all benefited from information technology such as EURODAC, which has facilitated their implementation (Broeders 2009; Schuster in this volume). In other words, the unification of Europe and the development of European policy have played an important role in attempting to manage migration flows. Agreements such as Schengen (1985) and especially the Dublin I/II regulations (1990 and 2003) give EU member states the necessary tools. Therefore a major change, in the European context since the 1970s, has been the increasing importance of the supranational tier in the production of irregular migration. In short, increased border controls have limited access to EU countries through regularized routes and have resulted in more irregular migration, certainly up until 2000 (Koser 2005).

Another contemporary change concerns the extent of irregular migration. While, in the 1970s, irregular migration was more of a phenomenon in the wealthier countries of the global north and west, it is now globally prevalent, as most irregular migration takes place between countries in the developing world (Koser 2005). A comparison of policies across time and space shows that, for almost all countries, irregular migration is seen as a 'problem' to solve. This can be explained by the fact that irregular migration is intrinsically related to immigration policy, border controls and definitions of citizenship by nation-states. It is not surprising, therefore, that the notion of 'clandestine migration' appeared for the first time in the nineteenth century when nation-states concretized and provided the legal tools to define legal and illegal mobility (Ngai 2004; Cvajner and Sciortino 2010). The debates on irregular migration show that nation-states still aim to protect a juridical membership and their territorial sovereignty. However, despite attempts to prevent irregular migration, it persists because, as Ngai notes, 'legislation cannot cover all permutations and eventualities' (2004, pp. 4–5). A consequence of this increased repression is the growing criminalization of irregular migration, as some of the papers in this issue demonstrate.

Despite increased immigration controls and greater surveillance, the overview on irregular migration policy provided by the papers in this special issue shows that states tend to adopt a pragmatic perspective, focusing on employers, criminals, migrant smugglers and agents and newcomers instead of promoting the continuous mass deportation of irregular migrant workers. This pragmatism marks what Joppke (1998) has called the liberal state's 'self-limited sovereignty', highlighting on the one hand the inability of governments to control immigration flows and the other hand the human rights that nation-states are entitled to provide to any human beings independently of their status, such as healthcare and education (Joppke 1998; Guiraudon 2001; Castles 2004; Cornelius 2005).

The final key area of change has been the form that irregular migration takes, which has altered in a number of ways since the 1970s. Irregular migration flows are no longer just related to labour migration. In the post-war context, irregular migrants were often guest-workers who regularized their situation of stay and work after they had been employed (Sinn, Kreienbrink and von Loeffelholz 2005). Irregular migrants were mainly from proximate countries: from Latin America to the US (Edwards 2006) and from Eastern or Southern Europe to Northern and Western Europe (Düvell 2008). In the European context, the expansion of the EU means that people from traditional migrant-sending countries from the south and east of Europe are now able to move freely within the EU zone and, if previously irregular, have been able to regularize their situation.

At the same time, barriers to Europe and the US have become, as already mentioned, greater for unskilled workers from outside these continents, making regular migration unlikely. As a consequence, the majority of irregular migrants today come from non-European countries, which also complicates the channels of irregular migration. The migration is longer, more expensive, can entail greater risks and for many necessitates the use of agents and smugglers for border crossing and documentation (Koser 2005; Van Liempt 2007). In other words, repressive policies have not prevented irregular migration, but have diversified its characteristics and modes of illegality (Triandafyllidou 2010). This diversification means that most countries, even non-traditional countries for immigration, are affected by irregular migration. This diversity has led to research in a number of areas, and these will be explored in the next section.

Studies of irregular migration: key issues and concepts

After becoming a prominent issue with the recruitment limitations in the US in 1924 and in the 1970s in Europe, irregular migration was neglected by the literature until the 1990s and especially the 2000s.[1] As highlighted by Portes (1978) and De Genova (2002) irregular migration has, for a long time, been approached as a problem, leading research to adopt a policy perspective and envisage solutions. Since the 1990s, researchers have tried to adopt a more comprehensive perspective. This research is usually based on geographically specific case studies exploring one dimension of policy, politics or experience, and theoretical accounts remain limited. We can distinguish four main focuses for research: taxonomies of irregularity, the making of irregularity, the social and demographic characteristics of irregular migrants and reflections on citizenship and membership. This section will examine the main themes that emerge from these bodies of work.

Taxonomies of irregularity

A number of studies have explored irregularity as a social construct, including the ways in which it is conceptualized, and have examined the ways in which its definition might vary according to the context. Anderson and Ruhs argue that irregularity may be 'a consequence of shifting state policies or of individual choices and opportunities' (2010, p. 177). For this reason the conceptualization of irregularity goes beyond the illegal/legal divide and instead represents a range of situations on a continuum between two ideal types. At one end of the spectrum are those who combine all types of irregularity (irregular entry, residence, work and illegal practices) while at the other end is the 'perfect' citizen (Düvell 2008, p. 490). Somewhere in between there are cases of 'semi-compliant' migrants who, for example, have overstayed their visa or are otherwise violating visa conditions, including students who work more hours than is allowed (Ruhs and Anderson 2010). These taxonomies lead authors to conclude that there exists a 'hierarchy of irregular statuses' (Cvajner and Sciortino 2010, p. 395), which helps to explain why some irregular migrants are deported while others are not. These taxonomies can also be generated from 'below'; while governments tend to use the term 'illegal' or 'clandestine' to define this population, advocacy groups mainly use the term 'undocumented migrants' or '*sans papiers/sin papeles*' to criticize their naturalization and denounce their criminalization, arguing that the only offence they commit is to contravene immigration policy (Anderson and Ruhs 2010; De Genova 2002).

The making of irregularity and policy responses

A second area of research and scholarship examines the production of irregularity and is pursued through policy analysis. Studies have explored immigration policies, identifying when and which national policies have affected the flows and stocks of irregular migration in given countries. More recently European projects such as Clandestino have aimed to provide crossed-national comparisons (Triandafyllidou 2010). The Clandestino research shows that, although all EU member states are affected by irregular migration and seek to harmonize their immigration policies in line with EU directives and recommendations, the ways in which individual states deal with their irregular populations varies. Spain demonstrates a high level of tolerance towards irregular migrants and irregular work, and regularizes the status of this population periodically. In contrast the Scandinavian countries currently have the most repressive policies. In Denmark, for instance, irregular migrants have no right to healthcare, but in principle health professionals have an ethical obligation to provide medical care in cases of emergency, though what is considered as an emergency can vary according to contexts. In addition, no formal arrangements are made to accept children at school (see, for instance, PICUM n.d.). Explanations for these differences are numerous and include path-dependency, countries' immigration traditions or colonial histories, their welfare levels and also the degree to which their economic contexts are more or less favourable to labour migration (Hollifield 2004; Schierup, Hansen and Castles 2006; Bade *et al.* 2007; Castles and Miller 2009).

Looking at solutions to irregular migration in individual nation-states, several studies have also reported and analysed the process of regularization and have made cross-national comparisons (Levinson 2005; Regine Project 2009). Moreover, some research explains why nation-states choose to regularize their irregular populations (Laubenthal 2007).

Social and demographic characteristics of irregular migrants

A number of empirical studies, discussed below, examine the numbers and profiles of irregular migrants, their everyday lives and their paths into irregularity.

Recent estimates show that, between 2000 and 2008, the number of irregular migrants resident in European countries decreased because of the increasingly draconian immigration controls described in the previous section, but also the enlargement of the EU and regularization programmes (Triandafyllidou 2010). In this context, research has focused on the hardship faced by irregular migrants, calling their situation a downward spiral because of: their 'rightlessness' (Krause 2008; Bloch 2010); their propensity to be involved in precarious work (Chimienti *et al.* 2003; Bloch, Sigona and Zetter 2009; Ruhs and Anderson 2010) even after a putative regularization (Goldring and Landolt 2011); poor housing (Bloch, Sigona and Zetter 2009); limited access to healthcare and increasing health problems due to poor housing and poor working conditions, their isolation and the stress caused by the constant fear of police raids and their need to remain hidden (Chimienti and Achermann 2007; Willen, 2007). This picture of irregular migrants' lives has led some authors to speak of them as sacrificed, stuck in limbo or 'ruined by modernity' (Beneduce 2008, p. 509).

However some, such as Anderson and Ruhs (2010), argue that a structural analysis of the living conditions of irregular migrants needs to be combined with analysis of their agency to avoid the risk of 'oversimplifying a vision of irregular migrants either as "victims" of exploitation or as "villains" who broke the laws' (Anderson and Ruhs 2010, p. 177). A number of scholars have already acknowledged the need to explore the ways in which irregular migrants cope with their vulnerable situation. Bloch, Sigona and Zetter show, for instance, that through a complex process some irregular migrants manage to adjust and adapt to their situation, 'shrugg[ing] off any resistance to the challenge presented by their status' (2009, p. 94). Chimienti and Achermann (2007) highlight how irregular migrants create routines to combat the uncertainty they are facing and seek resources with the hope of a better future. Coutin (2000) and Ellermann (2010) both analysed forms of subversion by irregular migrants that allow them to 'escape the state's reach'. For Ellermann (2010) the 'identity-stripping' of those irregular migrants who destroy or hide their IDs in order not to be deported is a form of resistance to the state, although she associates this form of resistance with James Scott's 'weapons of the weak'. This type of resistance is characterized by an 'implicit disavowal of the state' and a 'focus on immediate gains' (Scott 1985, p. 33) and such resistance draws more on tactics than on strategies (Wills *et al.* 2010). Despite the limits of these tactics, looking at agency allows us to see irregularity as something that can be envisaged by some groups as a resource in a particular context (Heyman and Smart 1999). These reflections, that combine an analysis of structure and agency, lead to a more theoretical account of citizenship, as we will discuss briefly in the next section.

Citizenship and membership

A range of theoretical accounts consider irregular migration through the lens of citizenship and vice versa. These scholars have analysed the transformative potential irregular migrants have for the notion of citizenship, looking at this population as agents of political change and defining rights by their enactment versus by preconceived scripts (Balibar 2004; Rancière 2004; Gordon 2007; Isin 2009; McNevin 2009).

This literature has the merit of having conceived new forms of membership, not limited to juridical or political concepts, and new ways to 'become political', placing subjectivities at the starting point of activism (Isin 2009). However, this literature tends to overestimate the decline of state power while legal status can be granted only by the state (Nyers 2003). It also runs the risk of silencing irregular migrants' voices and immediate needs by interpreting their collective action as aiming at structural changes (Chimienti and Solomos 2011). Our view is that, to provide a sensitive understanding of irregular migration, scholars need to combine a multilevel analysis, exploring irregular migrants' lived experiences, their interpretations and subjective experiences and their social and structural context, necessitating theoretically informed empirical studies.

Mapping the special issue

In this section we examine the content of the substantive papers of this volume, which provide a comparative framework and multi-level analysis. Although the papers are mainly empirically orientated, they offer tracks for theory-driven work. All the papers explore the interaction between policies and individual agency and yet they do it in different contexts and within different policy spheres: supranational, national and/or local. All the papers demonstrate the vulnerability of irregular migrants though at the same time they demonstrate tactics for survival, either individually or collectively. Finally, they also highlight that, although policies may have resulted in declining numbers of irregular migrants and have certainly made their lives more difficult, they have not brought an end to irregular flows.

The first three papers by Bloch, Sigona and Zetter, Rutherford and Chavez examine the reasons for migration, the everyday lives and the degree of agency among irregular migrants in different countries. Bloch, Sigona and Zetter explore the motives for migration and the routes through which irregular migrants are or become irregular by drawing on a qualitative study of 75 young undocumented migrants in England. A recurrent theme in Bloch, Sigona and Zetter's analysis is the argument that, despite irregular migrants' situation of vulnerability, they make choices and develop strategies to cope with an increasingly restrictive and punitive immigration regime.

Rutherford examines modes of exclusion and inclusion among Zimbabweans in South Africa and more specifically their ways of dealing with migration policy. Rutherford shows that modes of belonging depend on a range of structural and individual factors and that modes of belonging can take different forms. These different forms include humanitarian zones that offer respite for irregular migrants and thus constitute spaces where irregular migrants can develop some kind of attachment and belonging. Rutherford shows that, because of their situation of vulnerability, irregular migrants' agency and the forms of security they might find are necessarily ambivalent and always involve challenges.

Chavez also examines the strategies of irregular migrants in relation to policy. He analyses border-crossing strategies among undocumented and documented migrants crossing between Tijuana in Mexico and the US. Chavez explores the range of tactics developed by migrants to lessen the likelihood of being seen as violators when crossing borders. He also shows that granting entry, even to documented migrants, is a not an objective practice, but is a subjective and racialized procedure which obliges migrants to depict themselves as victims in order to generate pity and decrease the risk of officers taking away their visas.

The two next papers, by Chimienti and Laubenthal, explore the political changes provoked by irregular migration. Chimienti examines these changes through the analysis of collective action among irregular migrants. This includes the reasons for, and modes of, irregular migrants' mobilization in London, Paris and Copenhagen. Chimienti shows that irregular migrants' mobilizations take place in specific subjective and objective contexts. In the subjective context, it requires shared awareness among protestors of facing a common injustice. The objective context represents on the one hand the suffering provoked by the shift from a previous period of tolerance to repression and on the other hand opportunities, both structural and discursive.

The paper by Laubenthal tracks political changes in the area of irregular migration rights from the perspectives of international human rights discourses and local pressure. Laubenthal analyses the structural precondition of irregular migrants' access to education in Germany. She shows that irregular migrants' access to education, with other social rights, is influenced by forces at different levels of governance: the supranational level through human rights discourse and instruments and the subnational level through *Länder*. Laubenthal concludes that the federal structure of Germany influences measures in favour of irregular migrants' access to education.

The last two papers focus on national and supranational policies and their consequences for irregular migrants. The paper by Hagan, Mullis and Rodriguez analyses the expansion of US immigration policy enforcement and the influence of current US deportation measures on migrants' characteristics and lives. The paper argues that current policy criminalizes irregular migrants and shows the adverse effects that this criminalization has on the lives of these migrants.

The final paper by Schuster investigates the effects of Dublin II on Afghan migrants travelling through Greece to France. Schuster argues that Dublin II creates a process of illegalization by EU member states which essentializes migrants, depicting them as passive victims or criminals. Moreover, Schuster argues that Dublin I and II prevent people from seeking asylum, which is by definition unconstitutional and concludes that EU policy is seriously questionable from a human rights perspective.

Conclusion

This paper shows the continuous and changing patterns of irregular migration over time and space. Despite macro-changes that have included global economic crises, from the 1970s to the current one and increasingly repressive policies towards migrants from the global south and east, irregular migration has continued. This ongoing situation can be explained by the congruence of interests of economies, policies and individuals in both 'receiving' and 'sending' countries.

This continuity also highlights the remaining power of the national state, although it can be challenged by irregular migrants. On the one hand irregular migrants illustrate the changing meaning of citizenship by creating new forms of membership, not limited to juridical territoriality, and argue for a new conceptualization of citizenship that goes beyond nation-state definitions (Balibar 2004; Isin 2009). This perspective is also encouraged through international human rights instruments that set out to ensure that all people have access to human rights. However, on the other hand, and conflicting with access to human rights, is the dependency of their implementation on nation-states. Finally, as we have seen, international agreements do not merely promote human rights but have also limited them as illustrated by the case of Dublin regulations. The reality is that tangible changes to improve the situation of irregular migrants have been limited.

While the existing literature helps our understanding of irregular migration and the experiences of irregular migrants, from different perspectives, there are a number of questions that remain unanswered or only partially explored in the literature, some of which will become increasingly important in the coming years. First, little is known about the longer-term effects of irregularity. Longitudinal approaches are needed in order to have a greater understanding of the human and social costs of being an irregular migrant over time and of the effects of irregular migration on the economies and policies of 'receiving' and 'sending' countries. A longitudinal analysis should also include an exploration of the impact of migrants' agency, looking at the consequences of collective acts of resistance. A second important area of research is the analysis of the relationships between irregular migrations, nation-state allegiances, forms of belonging, citizenship and human rights. Linked to this is the role of civil society, not just in terms of perceptions about irregular migrants but also in terms of the role of civil society in the recognition or repression of this group. Finally, more comparative cross-national research would help to provide insights into similarities among and differences between destination countries. Such comparison needs to be based, as we have argued, on a multi-level analysis in order to provide a sensitive understanding of this phenomenon.

While many theoretical and empirical questions remain unanswered, the papers in this special issue begin to develop our understanding around the complexities of irregular migration across time and space, at the start of the twenty-first century. As a consequence, the papers provide new insights from which scholars can develop their theoretical and empirical questions.

Acknowledgements

Thanks to our colleagues in the Department of Sociology, City University London, especially Leah Bassel, John Solomos and Frank Webster. Thanks to Linnet Taylor for her input. Thanks to the contributors, discussants and other participants in the workshop that preceded this special issue.

Note

1. The number of special issues published in English since 2000 specifically on this topic attest to its current interest: *International Migration* 2007, vol. 45; *Social Science Information* 2008, vol. 47; *Ethics and International Affairs* 2008, vol. 22; *Population, Space and Place* 2010, vol. 16; *European Journal of Migration and Law* 2010, vol. 12 and so on; other special issues, dealing with mobility and citizenship, include several contributions on irregular migration; see, for instance, *European Journal of Social Theory* 2010, vol. 13; *Globalizations* 2011, vol. 8.

References

ANDERSON, B. and RUHS, M. 2010 'Guest editorial: researching illegality and labour migration', *Population, Space and Place*, vol. 16, no. 3, pp. 175–9

BADE, K. J., EMMER, P. C., LUCASSEN, L. and OLTMER, J. 2007 *Enzyklopädie Migration in Europa: vom 17. Jahrhundert bis zur Gegenwart*, Paderborn: Ferdinand Schöningh; Munich: Wilhelm Fink

BALIBAR, E. 2004 *We, the People of Europe? Reflections on Transnational Citizenship*, Princeton, NJ: Princeton University Press

BENEDUCE, R. 2008 'Undocumented bodies, burned identities: refugees, sans papiers, harraga: when things fall apart', *Social Science Information*, vol. 47, no. 4, pp. 505–27

BLOCH, A. 2010 'The right to rights? Undocumented migrants from Zimbabwe living in South Africa', *Sociology*, vol. 44, no. 2, pp. 233–50

BLOCH, A., SIGONA, N. and ZETTER, R. 2009 *'No Right to Dream': The Social and Economic Lives of Young Undocumented Migrants in Britain*, London: Paul Hamlyn Foundation

BROEDERS, D. 2009 *Breaking Down Anonymity: Digital Surveillance of Irregular Migrants in Germany and the Netherlands*, Amsterdam: Amsterdam University Press

CASTLES, S. 2004 'Why migration policies fail', *Ethnic and Racial Studies*, vol. 27, no. 2, pp. 205–27

CASTLES, S. and MILLER, M. J. 2009 [1993] *The Age of Migration: International Population Movements in the Modern World*, Basingstoke: Macmillan

CHIMIENTI, M. and ACHERMANN, 2007 'Coping strategies of precarious migrants in relation to personal health and health structures: the case of asylum seekers and undocumented migrants in Switzerland', in C. Björngren Cuadra and S. Cattacin (eds), *Difference Sensitivity from an Organisational Perspective*, Malmö: IMER, pp. 65–74

CHIMIENTI, M. and SOLOMOS, J. 2011 'Social movements of irregular migrants, recognition and citizenship', *Globalizations*, vol. 8, no. 1, forthcoming

CHIMIENTI, M., EFIONAYI-MÄDER, D. and FARQUET, R. 2003 *La répression du travail clandestin à Genève: Application et conséquences pour les personnes concernées*, Neuchâtel: Forum suisse pour l'étude des migrations et de la population

CORNELIUS, W. A. 2005 'Controlling "unwanted" immigration: lessons from the United States 1993–2004', *Journal of Ethnic and Migration Studies*, vol. 31, no. 4, pp. 775–94

COUTIN, S. B. 1993 *The Culture of Protest: Religious Activism and the U.S. Sanctuary Movement*, Boulder, CO: Westview

——— 2000 *Legalizing Moves: Salvadoran Immigrants' Struggle for U.S. Residency*, Ann Arbor: University of Michigan Press

CVAJNER, M. and SCIORTINO, G. 2010 'Theorizing irregular migration: the control of spatial mobility in differentiated societies', *European Journal of Social Theory*, vol. 13, no. 3, pp. 389–404

DE GENOVA, N. 2002 'Migrant "illegality" and deportability in everyday life', *Annual Review of Anthropology*, vol. 31, pp. 419–47

DÜVELL, F. 2008 'Clandestine migration in Europe', *Social Science Information*, vol. 47, no. 4, pp. 479–97

EDWARDS, J. R. 2006 *Two Sides of the Same Coin the Connection between Legal and Illegal Immigration: Backgrounder*, Washington, DC: Center for Immigration Studies

ELLERMANN, A. 2010 'Undocumented migrants and resistance in the liberal state', *Politics and Society*, vol. 38, no. 3, pp. 408–29

GOLDRING, L. and LANDOLT, P. 2011 'Caught in the work-citizenship matrix: the lasting effects of precarious legal status on work for Toronto immigrants', *Globalizations*, vol. 8, no. 1, forthcoming

GORDON, J. 2007 'Transnational labor citizenship', *Southern California Law Review*, vol. 80, no. 3, pp. 503–88

GUIRAUDON, V. 2001 'De-nationalizing control: analysing state responses to restraints on migration control', in V. Guiraudon and C. Joppke (eds), *Controlling a New Migration World*, London: Routledge, pp. 29–64

——— 2003 'Before the EU border: remote control of the huddled masses', in K. Groenendijk, E. Guild and P. Minderhoud (eds) *In Search of Europe's Borders*, The Hague: Kluwer, pp. 191–214

HEYMAN, J. M. C. and SMART, A. 1999 'States and illegal practices: an overview', in J. M. C. Heyman (ed.), *States and Illegal Practices*, New York: Berg, pp. 1–24

HOLLIFIELD, J. F. 1992 *Immigrants, Markets and States: The Political Economy of Post-war Europe*, Cambridge, MA: Harvard University Press

——— 2004 'The emerging migration state', *International Migration Review*, vol. 38, no. 3, pp. 885–912

INTERNATIONAL ORGANISATION FOR MIGRATION/ILO 2004 *Towards a Fair Deal for Workers in the Global Economy*, Report 4, International Conference, 92nd Session ILO, Geneva

ISIN, E. F. 2009 'Citizenship in flux: the figure of the activist citizen', *Subjectivity*, vol. 29, no. 1, pp. 367–88

JOPPKE, C. 1998 'Why liberal states accept unwanted immigration', *World Politics*, vol. 50, no. 2, pp. 266–93

JORDAN, B. and DÜVELL, F. 2002 *Irregular Migration: The Dilemmas of Transnational Mobility*, Cheltenham: Edward Elgar

KOSSER, K. 2005 *Irregular Migration, State Security and Human Security*, Geneva: Global Commission on International Migration

——— 2010 'Dimensions and dynamics of irregular migration', *Population, Space and Place*, vol. 16, no. 3, pp. 181–93

KRAUSE, M. 2008 'Undocumented migrants: an Arendtian perspective', *European Journal of Political Theory*, vol. 7, no. 3, pp. 331–48

LAUBENTHAL, B. 2007 'The emergence of pro-regularization movements in Western Europe', *International Migration*, vol. 45, no. 3, pp. 101–33

LEVINSON, A. 2005 *The Regularisation of Unauthorized Migrants: Literature Survey and Country Case Studies*, Oxford: COMPAS

MCNEVIN, A. 2009 'Contesting citizenship: irregular migrants and strategic possibilities for political belonging', *New Political Science*, vol. 31, no. 2, pp. 163–81

NGAI, M. M. 2004 *Impossible Subject: Illegal Aliens and the Making of Modern America*, Princeton, NJ, and Oxford: Princeton University Press

NYERS, P. 2003 'Abject cosmopolitanism: the politics of protection in the anti-deportation movement', *Third World Quarterly*, vol. 24, no. 6, pp. 1069–93

PICUM n.d. *Basic Social Rights: Country Case Study: Denmark*, http://www.picum.org/article/basic-social-rights-denmark [Accessed 17 April 2010]

PORTES, A. 1978 'Toward a structural analysis of illegal (undocumented) immigration', *International Migration Review*, vol. 12, no. 4, pp. 469–84

RANCIÈRE, J. 2004 'Who is the subject of the rights of man', *South Atlantic Quarterly*, vol. 103, nos. 2–3, pp. 297–310

REGINE PROJECT 2009 *Regularisations in Europe: Study on Practices in the Area of Regularisation of Illegally Staying Third-Country Nationals in the Member States of the EU*, Final Report, January, Vienna: ICMPD

RUHS, M. and ANDERSON, B. 2010 'Semi-compliance and illegality in migrant labour markets: an analysis of migrants, employers and the state in the UK', *Population, Space and Place*, vol. 16, no. 3, pp. 195–211

SCHIERUP, C.-U., HANSEN, P. and CASTLES, S. 2006 *Migration, Citizenship and the European Welfare State: A European Dilemma*, Oxford: Oxford University Press

SCOTT, J. 1985 *Weapons of the Weak: Everyday Forms of Peasant Resistance*, New Haven, CT: Yale University Press

SINN, A., KREIENBRINK, A and VON LOEFFELHOLZ, H. D. 2005 *Illegally Resident Third-Country Nationals in Germany: Policy Approaches, Profile and Social Situation*, Nürenberg: Bundesamt für Migration und Flüchtlinge

TRIANDAFYLLIDOU, A. (ed.) 2010 *Irregular Migration in Europe: Myths and Realities*, Farnham: Ashgate

VAN LIEMPT, I. 2007 *Navigating Borders: Inside Perspectives on the Process of Human Smuggling into the Netherlands*, Amsterdam: Amsterdam University Press

WALTERS, W. 2006 'Border/control', *European Journal of Social Theory*, vol. 9, no. 2, pp. 187–203

WILLEN, S. S. 2007 'Toward a critical phenomenology of "illegality": state power, criminalization, and abjectivity among undocumented migrant workers in Tel Aviv, Israel', *International Migration*, vol. 45, no. 3, pp. 8–36

WILLS, J., DATTA, K., EVANS, Y., HERBERT, J., MAY, J. and MCILWAINE, C. 2010 *Global Cities at Work: New Migrant Divisions of Labour*, London: Pluto

Migration routes and strategies of young undocumented migrants in England: a qualitative perspective

Alice Bloch, Nando Sigona and Roger Zetter

Abstract

Based on data from in-depth qualitative interviews with young undocumented migrants from Brazil, China, Ukraine, Zimbabwe and Kurds from Turkey, this article explores the entry strategies used by young people in relation to the UK immigration system and their undocumented status. Against a brief account of Britain's regime, the paper first examines why and how these migrants come to the UK and the ways in which they entered the country. Second, the paper explores strategies in relation to immigration status and considers: the use of different immigration statuses; the role of the asylum system in their strategies including as an attempt to regularize status or as a route to becoming undocumented when refused asylum. Finally, the paper examines the extent to which these young migrants have agency in their efforts to negotiate the complex and exclusionary immigration and asylum regime.

This article explores the entry strategies used by young people in relation to the UK immigration system and their undocumented status. Drawing upon the accounts of seventy-five young undocumented migrants, it investigates the tension between the 'migration project', which relies on existing social networks and reflects sedimented migratory histories (Brettel and Hollifield 2007; Castles and Miller 2009) and the opportunities and constraints defined by specific immigration regimes (Koopmans and Statham 2000; Zimmermann 2009).

Recent scholarship has pointed out how migration studies literature has often neglected the migratory experiences of children and young people and has paid limited attention to the interplay between age and migrants' decision-making (Giner 2007; O'Connell Davidson and Farrow 2007; Bhabha 2008). This article is a contribution to filling this gap. It offers a detailed account of the complex interplay of youth and other key factors in shaping young migrants' agency and the way in which they negotiate and move between different statuses in the context of increased immigration controls and severely diminished opportunities for non-EU low-skilled migrants to enter the UK in a regularized way (Zetter *et al.*, 2003).

Background: controlling immigration

Since the 1905 Aliens Act, Britain has controlled and regulated immigration. From their inception, immigration control and immigration policy have been closely linked to social welfare and employment (Harvey 2002), becoming more overtly racialized in the early 1960s when primary migration from New Commonwealth citizens was curtailed (Solomos 2003).

In the last twenty years a new era of international migration has had profound impacts on the political landscape of the UK. While the unprecedented rise in the numbers of asylum seekers arriving spontaneously dominated the agenda for much of this period, this category of migrant cannot easily be separated from wider processes and patterns of economic migration facilitated by increasing global mobility as well as by European enlargement. With the aim of 'managing' these different migratory processes, immigration and asylum acts have followed each other in rapid succession since the early 1990s, such that legal entry, particularly for some categories of migrants, has become extremely difficult (Sales 2007). As a consequence migrants, including some asylum seekers, are forced to take ever more difficult, dangerous and costly journeys (Koser 2005) and to remain clandestine and hidden on arrival. Illegality, De Genova validly notes, 'is the product of immigration laws' (2002, p. 439).

Irregular migration is a feature of all the most developed states and is high on policy agendas, particularly in relation to border controls. Much of the early scholarship in this area emerged from the US and focused on irregular labour migration from Mexico to the US (Chavez 1994; De Genova 2002). More recently from a European perspective, the restrictions on accessing the asylum process and the curtailment of regular migration routes have required migrants to use irregular and undocumented means of entry to accomplish the varied motives and aspirations for their migration project. The 'asylum-migration' nexus and the 'asylum-development' nexus are used to capture the variation and complexity of international migration (Castles and Van Hear 2005). Moreover, status is not static: people move between different statuses with varying degrees of agency and expedience (Jordan and Düvell 2002; Anderson and Rogaly 2005).

While states are concerned with controlling migration and in particular undocumented immigration and undocumented migrants, they also tacitly accept these migrants because they offer a cheap and readily disposable supply of labour without social and welfare costs to the state (Castles 2000). In consequence there are increasingly large numbers of undocumented migrants, without civil or social rights living in wealthier states. Given the hidden nature of this population, reliable evidence about numbers does not exist. In the UK, using the 2001 Census, the Home Office estimates that the *unauthorized* (i.e. not necessarily the same as *undocumented*) population lay between 430,000 and 570,000 (Home Office 2005, p. 5; see also Vollmer 2008). Gordon *et al.* (2009) reviewed and updated the Home Office figure, adding an estimate of UK-born children of irregular migrants. This study gives a central estimate of 725,000 irregular migrants at the end of 2007, two thirds of whom are based in London. The numbers therefore are sizeable though little is known about the daily lives and experiences of such irregular immigrants or how they position themselves in the receiving country.

However, previous research shows that, for many undocumented migrants, marginalization and uncertainty are a way of life which has been exacerbated by increasing campaigns by different governments in developed countries to selectively identify and deport those in breach of immigration controls (see, for example, Bloch and Schuster 2005; Willen 2007). Yet, despite all the restrictions and inherent vulnerability, substantial numbers of migrants come, or become, undocumented, choosing to remain hidden from the gaze of the state. It is in this context that the question to be asked is: despite all the controls and restrictions, why and how do so many young people migrate to Britain in what seem to be very unpropitious circumstances?

Methodology

This paper draws on data from in-depth qualitative interviews with seventy-five undocumented migrants, thirty-five women and forty men, aged 18 to 31 living in Birmingham, London and Manchester or the surrounding areas.[1] Interviews were carried out with sixteen young migrants from each of Brazil, China and Zimbabwe, fourteen with Kurds from Turkey and thirteen with Ukrainians. All participants at the time of interview had no right of residence in the UK.

The research design was informed by a scoping study (Bloch *et al.* 2007) that provided the research team with insights into the different labour-market characteristics, types of employment and welfare provisions for undocumented migrants, as well as highlighting the importance of exploring the specificities of migration histories, community formation and settlement patterns. It also informed our understanding of 'youth' as a culturally specific and socially constructed concept. Youth is a social process, not simply a biological or demographic status, mediated by the tension between the social significance of age, which gives young people a common status, the significance of other social divisions and the multiplicity of competing, and sometimes contradictory, discursive regimes championed by different social groups (Hall 1992; Rose 1996; Wyn and White 1997; Rattansi and Phoenix 2005).

Informed by these insights, the choice of participants' countries of origin enabled us to capture variations as much as commonalities in the experiences of young undocumented migrants.

Participants were accessed through a broad range of social networks and gate-keepers, which ensured variety and diversity of migratory networks and experiences. Interviews were carried out between July and November 2008 by experienced field-workers with relevant language fluency for each community. To ensure anonymity and confidentiality, pseudonyms were used and all potential identifiers were removed or modified in the interview transcripts.[2]

Reasons for migration

People migrate for complex reasons and often have mixed motives, both for their migration and for their migration destination (Castles and Miller 2009). Migration can be an individual decision or part of a household survival strategy with migrants sending remittances to family members in the country of origin or elsewhere in the diaspora. Global inequality, conflict, oppression, lack of sustainable livelihoods and uneven development all contribute to the reasons why people migrate, although for some the impetus might also include, or be due to, social and kinship networks, or just the opportunity to experience a new culture, learn a new language or to have an adventure (Castles 2000; Mai 2007).

Our research, while corroborating this complex picture emphasizes how the experiences, motivations and aspirations of young undocumented migrants must be framed and understood in relation to their 'youth' (Hall 1992; Rose 1996) and the circumstances in their country of origin. Migrants' accounts powerfully relate this conjuncture between the drivers of migration and the 'youth project'. Migration represents, for many young undocumented migrants, a rite of passage in the transition to adulthood, and to a new social role (Margolis 1994). It is also a formative and transformative experience which shapes their present identity and their actual relationships with peers and society in general (Rattansi and Phoenix 2005; Mai 2007).

The principal migration drivers, in relation to country of origin, are closely linked to the prevalent political and/or economic situation. Among Zimbabweans the decision to migrate was often made by parents or was a collective family decision. Political problems in Zimbabwe were the main reason in cases where the individual was directly engaged in political activity or had family members who had been involved, indirectly threatening the safety of the young person. In the case of Bob, who had been involved in information dissemination for the Movement for Democratic Change (MDC), and had been tortured in Zimbabwe, the decision to leave was simply, he said, 'because I feared for my life. I was arrested several times' (Bob, 31, male, Zimbabwean).

Around half of the Zimbabwean interviewees came to join a family member who was already in Britain, with seven coming as teenagers, so for these young people the decision was made for them. In this respect Zimbabweans in our sample stand out from young migrants in other groups, because, almost without exception, they came as young adults and of their own volition. Ray arrived in Britain when he was 13 and his migration was driven by his mother, though it was also based on the situation in Zimbabwe as the following shows. 'I think my mum had a vision, there was problems, clearly it wasn't an environment conducive to us being there politically, it just . . . you have to look at the country to look at how unstable it is' (Ray, 21, male, Zimbabwean). For many young people from Zimbabwe return is not a realistic possibility and so the situation in their country of origin affects their experiences in Britain as it also does for young Kurdish people.

For Kurdish young undocumented migrants, the discrimination they experienced as a minority group, such as police oppression and violence against them and fear due to their political activities and views, were evident in their reasons for leaving. Amed, for instance, said that 'my reason to come to this country is my life was in danger' (29, male, Kurd from Turkey). Among some young men, avoiding military service was also an important reason because they knew that if they were in the Turkish army they would be stationed in Kurdistan. Firat who has been in Britain for seven years and was politically active prior to his migration felt that he had to leave suddenly. For Firat, avoiding military service was also part of his motive for migration, summed up when he said: 'There is a war in Turkey and that war is against Kurds. . . . How I can fight against my own people? How can you fire bullets against your own people?' (30, male, Kurd from Turkey).

The migratory decisions of Chinese young people were much more economically motivated than among Zimbabweans and Kurds. For the most part migration had been a personal decision of the young person but was often taken in the context of economic considerations in relation to family and household circumstances as Huadi Zhang describes:

> We ran a small business and we made a loss. . . . Our family ran a small brickyard and sold machines. . . . If I didn't go abroad the family would never be able to clear the debts . . . so I had to take a chance. That's why I chose to smuggle myself out. The majority of people who chose to smuggle themselves out are all those who had no alternative but to do so. (29, male, Chinese)

One of the problems young people face is the huge debts they accrue to pay the snakeheads to smuggle them out of China. Gao Zeng, who has been in Britain for two years and eight months, reflects on his situation:

> I thought I'd better go abroad to earn money. But the money spent for me to smuggle myself out was quite something, it was already something in the range of 300,000 Yuan [roughly £20,000]. I had to borrow bits and bobs. . . . I haven't paid back the debts yet. (24, male, Chinese)

Ukrainians were, for the most part, also motivated to migrate for economic reasons though the decision was usually an individual one. Rita, who joined her husband in Britain, did not describe joining her husband as her main motivation for migration, or even claim that she was looking to settle in Britain, although she has now been here for more than three years. Instead she says that she came to Britain 'simply to earn and return' (29, female, Ukrainian). For a few Ukrainians, learning English, having an adventure, fulfilling a long-held dream and travel were also the reasons for their migration.

Echoing these social drivers of migration but in contrast to the other country-of-origin groups, the migration circumstances of young people from Brazil were more obviously motivated by social considerations. Some came to join a partner, a relative or friends, such as Eduardo who came mainly to join his girlfriend. 'I came because I had a girlfriend who came here. . . . I came mainly because of her but also because of money, of course to make money, to change my life, you know to change a bit' (23, male, Brazilian).

For others, migration was an adventure, allowing exposure to another culture; for some it enabled them to learn a new language. A few came with the specific reason of developing skills or working to save money, such as Celso. 'I came with the aim of working and studying, learn the English language you know' (28, male, Brazilian).

The 'migration rationale' of Brazilians was more individualistic, rarely linked to a family decision and far less closely driven by economic or political factors in their country of origin compared to the other four groups.

Entering Britain: choice or chance?

Research has explored the reasons why asylum seekers apply for asylum in particular countries. This includes former colonial-imperial links as a determinant (Havinga and Böcker 1999) though more recent research notes new geographies of migration where asylum seekers arrive in countries without former colonial links (Koser and Pinkerton 2002). Instead, perceptions of asylum systems and human rights, smuggling routes and social networks shape destination countries (Robinson and Segrott, 2002; Gilbert and Koser, 2006).

In this study, some arrived as asylum seekers or entered the asylum system while others had mixed or different motivations for migration, notably economic and/or social. Increasingly restrictive immigration controls limit the opportunities for low-skilled people to enter Britain using a regularized route and this trend is reflected in the strategies of some young migrants who relied on agents, smugglers or traffickers to organize their journeys and, for some, their forged documents. Others entered the UK on visas and then over-stayed or became 'clandestine' if their asylum cases had been refused. County of origin affected migration routes, entry strategies, the propensity to seek asylum and aspirations in terms of what the young people wanted to achieve in the UK, attitudes about return and about deportation.

Figure 1 summarizes the ways in which people entered the UK by country of origin. Of the 75 interviewees 28 entered on forged documents or without documents. Chinese, Kurds and Ukrainians used these means most frequently. For many who used forged documents, smugglers or agents were used to acquire the documents, while others travelled using forged documents and once at the border claimed asylum. Twenty five entered as tourists or visitors and this route was used most by Zimbabweans and Brazilians. Nine had student visas, seven sought asylum at the port of entry and two had temporary work permits.

Most young people made a deliberate decision to come to Britain and targeted it as a destination. Perceptions of economic opportunities, social and kinship networks, language and culture and, among Kurdish young people, perceptions about what Britain offered in terms of cultural freedom, the asylum system and a good human rights record were all influential. A small minority would have preferred a different destination and Britain was their second choice. For others it appears that Britain was more feasible to get to or it was the

Figure 1 *Entry routes by country of origin*
Source: *Bloch, Sigona and Zetter (2009, p. 16)*

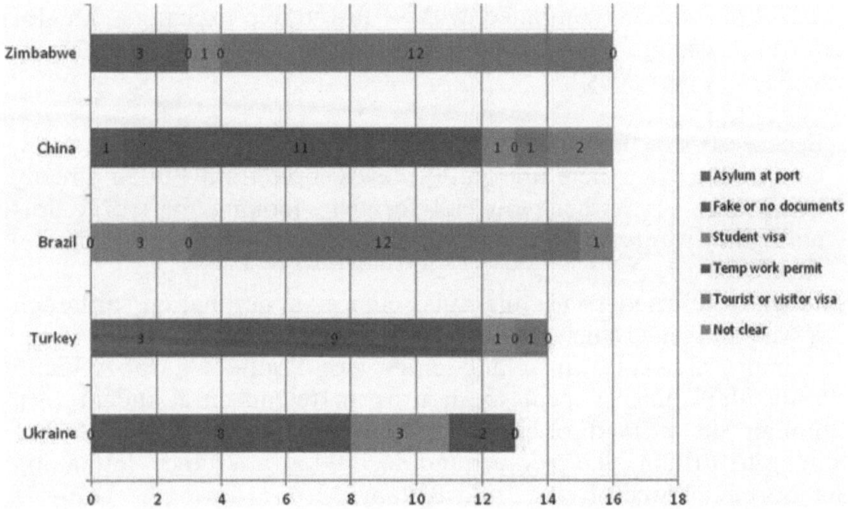

destination selected by smugglers and thus where they happened to end up.

The diversity of factors motivating the decision to come to Britain was also strongly linked, among some country of origin groups, to pre-migration experiences and circumstances. Britain was the first choice among most Chinese, Kurdish and Ukrainian migrants. Brazilians tended to come to Britain because friends or partners were also coming or already in the UK, while for others it was an interest in the language and culture. Bernardo (26, male, Brazilian), for instance, was looking for a change in his life and, as he already had a friend in London, it seemed like an obvious choice.

For Kurdish and Chinese young people, Britain was deliberately chosen as a destination because of perceptions about its human rights credentials and economic prosperity. For Kurds, Britain was thought to offer safety, asylum, cultural and linguistic freedom and good human rights. As Botan stated, 'I knew this country set great value on human rights. People can use whatever language they want' (29, male, Kurd from Turkey).

Some came to Britain from other European countries because they were advised Britain offered more possibilities, as the following shows:

> I wanted to stay in Belgium but I was told that the rules are stricter and conditions are difficult to stay in Belgium for somebody like me . . . I was advised to think about France and the UK . . . we started looking for an option to get to the UK. Three days later we were in the UK. (Necirwan, 30, male, Kurd from Turkey)

For most young undocumented Chinese migrants, Britain was the planned destination because its then strong economy offered employment opportunities combined with a favourable exchange rate for remitting earnings. Pre-existing social networks were also a factor as Yao Xiamin describes:

> Because firstly the exchange rate of the pound is higher. Secondly, here in the UK, there are quite a few people from Fujian already living here . . . so when you call for help looking for work, normally they would be quite willing to assist you. (25, female, Chinese)

Smuggling affected some migrants' choice of destination, although this was neither exclusive to the Chinese community nor was it the principal means of transit and entry (see Figure 1). Yao Xiamin (25, female, Chinese) spent six months in Ireland on a student visa, although she worked rather than studied while in Ireland, before coming to Britain. She paid around £6,700 for 'assistance' in making the journey between Ireland and Britain.

Most young undocumented migrants from Ukraine said that England was the intended destination because of the earning potential. Fedia, for example, says that 'I knew before that in England you can earn money' (29, male, Ukrainian). Sergiy had always been interested in England but would have preferred America. It was a pragmatic decision to travel to England: 'To go unofficially, it was only possible to go to Britain. It was simple to go to Britain. Basically I liked Britain too. And it was more realistic to come here' (27, male, Ukrainian).

Among Zimbabweans Britain was for the most part the preferred destination. For some it was a consequence of pre-existing family ties, exemplified most among the young Zimbabwean migrants who came to Britain as teenagers, such as Theo who arrived aged 12 and 'did not know anything because I was a kid' (19, male, Zimbabwean). For most Britain was not a dream but just an obvious choice, not part of a longer-term strategy. Colin illustrates this when he says, 'Personally I never really thought about it. I knew I had family here, but I never really said to myself "I want to come to Britain"' (23, male, Zimbabwean). However, the exception to this was Tanaka who described coming to Britain as 'a dream come true' (22, female, Zimbabwean).

Immigration strategies

People move in and out of different statuses – some enter in an irregular way, regularize their status through the asylum system and then become undocumented when their asylum case is refused. As

Cvajner and Sciortino note, 'irregularity is a status that may be both attained and left behind in different ways' (2010, p. 214) and as such, they argue, undocumented migration can take a number of different paths. This mobility was apparent in our study where seven young undocumented migrants had claimed asylum at the border and twelve had claimed asylum since being in the UK – two Chinese, six Kurds from Turkey and four Zimbabweans. All have had their asylum claims rejected and are now undocumented migrants. Others enter in a regularized way, for example, on a visa and then over-stay their visa and in so doing become undocumented. In this section, we explore some of the ways in which young people have become undocumented or moved between statuses. Our data reflect the assertion by Anderson and Ruhs (2010) that irregular migration and migrant decision-making need to be examined within the context of personal biographies and structural and economic processes. With that in mind it is not surprising that there were clear differences between and sometimes within country-of-origin groups.

The routes and strategies among Brazilians were relatively uncomplicated. Most entered the UK on tourist visas, preparing in advance for immigration at the airport by booking hotels, return flights and demonstrating the necessary financial resources to travel in the country. However, most Brazilians were also clear that this was their strategy for entry and that they planned to stay for a period of time and work in breach of their entry visa. Eduardo (23, male, Brazilian) told the immigration officer that 'I came to travel' but went on to state in the interview 'I had my return ticket, everything' because he was aware that the immigration officer would want evidence that he was planning to return to Brazil, though Eduardo like others knew he was going to stay.

Once in the UK Brazilians tend to buy forged ID and National Insurance numbers that enable them to work. Five are investigating and collecting evidence of their European ancestry in an effort to obtain citizenship of an EU member state and thus entitlement to reside in the UK, while two have got married to EU nationals although not, they say, to obtain residency.

Among the thirteen Ukrainians interviewed, seven entered Britain on forged documents and one was smuggled in without any documents. Lesya describes the process as follows: 'I came completely on someone else's passport that has a visa. Simply my picture was glued in [it]. And that's it. I came in about two hours. By a plane. That's how I came' (29, female, Ukrainian). Like Brazilians, those who came in on visas or permits had intended to over-stay and this was part of their strategy, as Semen describes: 'My visa simply ran out. . . . Those who returned after this visa have never been re-admitted to England. . . . I knew what I am doing' (28, male, Ukraine). Talking about her agricultural working visa

Victoria makes a similar point. 'I was told that an agricultural visa is not renewable. This visa was for three months and I didn't even think to go back home, because in three months I didn't even make enough money to pay my friend back for my trip' (24, female, Ukraine). Unlike Brazilians, young undocumented migrants from Ukraine were not trying to regularize their status. A few had acquired forged documents for work purposes and one had tried to get her visa extended but they were not proactive in terms of strategies.

Chinese young people were most likely to enter the UK with forged documents or without any documents having employed the services of smugglers (eleven out of sixteen). Some made very long and difficult journeys, such as Xiao Xue, a man of 21, who had been in the UK for two and a half years. The journey to the UK took nearly a year and involved travelling by lorry, boat and by foot.

> *Xiao Xue*: We stayed in all sorts of places along the way. . . . We travelled by all sorts of vehicles . . . sometimes lorry, sometimes boat, except airplane. At one point we had to walk for two days and two nights. We climbed over snow-capped mountains, too, where we were stopped by the border-guards at the border. They shouted "stop! stop!" But nobody stopped. We were panicked and fled. Shots were fired to the sky.
> *Interviewer*: They fired shots?...How dangerous . . . .And you didn't stop running?
> *Xiao Xue*: Had we stopped running, we wouldn't be here now.

Most Chinese young undocumented migrants did not have strategies to regularize their status although two have claimed asylum in the UK and one plans to claim asylum. Four, had chosen not to claim asylum because they worried about being detained and deported as the following quote shows.

> We had thought of claiming for asylum. They say that you'd get lots of benefits you're given asylum-status. But later they say that you might be detained if you claim asylum. They say that if you go to claim asylum, you might be detained and then sent home. Who wants to risk being sent home? (Zhu Chen, female, 25, China)

Among Kurdish and Zimbabwean young people seeking asylum, not surprisingly, has been much more prevalent than among the other groups due to the circumstances in their countries of origin. For some this is the principal motive for migration; for others it is the inability to return. Eleven out of fourteen Kurdish interviewees had had their asylum cases refused. Three had sought asylum at the port of entry and eight had been in-country applicants though applying shortly after arrival. One young woman, Avashin, made the decision not to seek asylum as she was scared of being refused and then deported, saying that 'I was scared because I thought if they reject my asylum application I might get . . . sent back immediately' (female, 29, Kurd from Turkey).

Among most Kurds from Turkey there has been a recognized strategy in seeking status. The young migrants enter the UK in an irregular way, seek asylum and therefore have a status in the UK, albeit with limited and temporary rights, and then become undocumented again when their cases have been refused. Part of the problem faced by young undocumented migrants when they enter the asylum system is their own lack of knowledge alongside, from their point of view, the poor legal advice or assistance they are given. Cihan, for example came to the UK five years ago using a fake passport and applied for asylum on arrival.

> There were a lot of new laws at that time . . . about asylum seekers, about students. . . . I went to my solicitor . . . he didn't do anything, he told me I could apply . . . when I applied I was supposed to get a application form but I did not receive it I got rejected, my lawyer said he was surprised that so I got rejected so quickly, then I signed a form and was given a court date, I went to court, the jury was fine, I thought everything went well. . . . But I got rejected . . . they didn't ask me any questions, but it wasn't a fair rejection, they only asked me a few questions, my name and when I came here, the barrister spoke a little about me, he had no evidence in his hand. (23, male, Kurd from Turkey)

The impact on Kurdish young people who have had their asylum cases refused can be substantial. Very real fear of deportation permeates their everyday lives and experiences, as described by Rojda, a young woman of 22 who has been in the UK for four years.

> I would like to live in this country and have the rights to be available to live here. I don't want to go back to Turkey. I don't want to be arrested or tortured again. I like to live, be alive. Being undocumented destroys my psychology. I don't have any paper; I can't stay in this house. I can't even sleep...I always hear from the other people how Home Office walks into the houses and takes people away to deport them to their countries. (22, female, Kurd from Turkey)

Some Zimbabweans also fear deportation and, like Kurdish young people, have moved between statuses. Zimbabweans for the most part entered the UK in a regular way either on tourist/visitor visas or as students, as Figure 1 shows (thirteen out of sixteen). Many of those who came into the UK on visas arrived before 2002 which was when visa restrictions were placed on those travelling to the UK and so they obtained their visas at the UK airport of entry. Three applied for asylum at the port of entry and an additional five had been through the asylum process in the UK. Others, though, have not applied. They either over-stay their visa or change to a student visa and then over-stay that.

A few of the Zimbabweans interviewed had very complex immigration status trajectories with greater mobility between different statuses. Suku, for example, was 30 at the time of the interview and had been in the UK for eight and a half years. She entered the country on a six-month visa and then extended it to a three-year student visa. She then lost her passport and bought a Zambian passport with an 'Indefinite Leave to Remain' stamp. She was arrested when her work place was raided and placed in a detention centre. She subsequently claimed asylum, was rejected and is now living as an undocumented migrant.

Among those who came to the UK as children, there is the added complexity of their parents' undocumented status and/or status as refused asylum seekers. This underscores their determination to remain hidden from the authorities. Theo, for example, was a dependant in his mother's asylum application which was rejected. Other young people lacked any knowledge of their situation for a number of years. Ray who came to Britain aged 13 and was told to say he was coming on holiday on arrival, describes how he first realized about his status.

> Got to 16 er I think that was the first wake up call. All the kids were talking about "Oh! I just got me NI card in the post". Why didn't my NI card come through the post?... because obviously I'm not in the system... and then since then it's just really unravelled. Really... er OK this is the status! [You] need this thing called status. (21, male, Zimbabwean)

The Zimbabweans who arrived in Britain as young teenagers to join family members tend to rely on these adult family members to negotiate and deal with the immigration system. They have little knowledge of their situation or what the possibilities might be for them. However, their lack of papers and disempowerment have a huge impact on their young lives. When Theo, who was 19 at the time of the interview and had been in the UK for more than six years, was asked about the impact of being undocumented on his life he responded, 'It's affected everything... I can't do anything... I just sit and rot' (19, male, Zimbabwean).

Conclusion

Our examination of the reasons for migration and the strategies used by young undocumented migrants in relation to their entry to the UK and their movement between different statuses shows the intersection of a number of different factors. The reasons for migration vary and country of origin impacts strongly with these variations. For some migrants, especially Zimbabwean, Kurdish and Chinese young people, the situation in their country of origin politically and/or economically, alongside perceptions about what the UK could offer, was a strong motivator to migrate and to choose the UK as a destination. The notable exception was those Zimbabweans who arrived in Britain as teenagers and had little or no agency over their migration. For others, especially those from Brazil and Ukraine, relationships, being young, having an adventure and the desire to accumulate capital assets for their future were much more evident in their narratives (cf. Margolis 1994).

Strategies and migration routes result from negotiating the tension between the 'migration project', and the constraints and possibilities offered by the immigration regime (Cvajner and Sciortino 2010). While for some young undocumented migrants, the routes into the UK and strategies for remaining in the UK as an undocumented migrant are 'rational' and pre-planned, for others becoming undocumented is something that happens to them or is an inevitable consequence of other factors. These might include the infeasibility of returning to a country of origin where they would, or might, be subjected to discrimination, human rights abuses, political oppression and/or a lack of sustainable livelihoods or because they would be unable to repay the debts they incurred for the migration journey.

The data show how being undocumented intersects with migration and immigration trajectories, as well as the motivations and experiences of young migrants. Some groups tend to arrive in an 'irregular' way, notably Kurdish and Chinese migrants. Others arrive on visas with the intention of over-staying or they over-stay as their lives develop and unfold in the UK in unanticipated ways, while some arrive and claim asylum at the port of entry or in country, but are then refused. The strategies used and the decisions made are directly correlated with pre-migration experiences and the prevailing situation in the country of origin. For some young migrants, trying to regularize status is a risky strategy that would raise their visibility with the authorities, while others see little need to regularize their status. Those who have been through the asylum system are most vulnerable, and it is only on refusal that they feel they have no other option but to remain as undocumented migrants due to the risk and fear of deportation and return. This was especially the case among young

Kurdish migrants but also among some Zimbabweans. Others had decided not to enter the asylum system for fear of having cases refused with the subsequent risk of detention and deportation.

In conclusion, the paper shows the complexity and variations in decisions to migrate but also in terms of the agency young people show over their immigration status. Some know from the outset that they will be, or will become, undocumented while others simply become undocumented as their lives unfold in ways that are incompatible with their official immigration status. Those whose asylum cases have failed feel that they have no other realistic options. However, most of the seventy-five young undocumented migrants interviewed in this research aspired to regularize their immigration status, although for most this was a pipe dream. In the meantime, for many, life was about existing and surviving outside the public gaze and in a state of limbo (Bloch, Sigona and Zetter 2009).

Notes

1. This paper draws on research funded by the Social Justice Programme of the Paul Hamlyn Foundation

2. For a detailed discussion of the methodology, see Appendix 1 in Bloch, Sigona and Zetter (2009).

References

ANDERSON, B. and ROGALY, B. 2005 *Forced Labour and Migration to the UK*, Oxford: Centre for Migration, Policy and Society TUC

ANDERSON, B. and RUHS, M. 2010 'Guest editorial: researching illegality and labour migration', *Population, Space and Place*, vol. 16, no. 3, pp. 175–9

BHABHA, J. 2008 'Independent children, inconsistent adults: international child migration and the legal framework', *Innocenti Discussion Paper No. 08/3*, UNICEF

BLOCH, A. and SCHUSTER, L. 2005 'At the extremes of exclusion: deportation, detention and dispersal', *Ethnic and Racial Studies*, vol. 28, no. 3, pp. 491–512

BLOCH, A., SIGONA, N. and ZETTER, R. 2009 *'No Right to Dream': The Social and Economic Lives of Young Undocumented Migrants in Britain*, London: Paul Hamlyn Foundation.

BLOCH, A., ZETTER, R., SIGONA, N. and ASHAMI, M. 2007 *Research into Undocumented Migrants: Scoping Study Report*, London: Paul Hamlyn Foundation

BRETTEL, C. B. and HOLLIFIELD, J. (eds) 2007 *Migration Theory: Talking across Disciplines*, 2nd edn, New York and London: Routledge

CASTLES, S. 2000 'International migration at the beginning of the twenty-first century: global trends and issues', *International Social Science Journal*, vol. 165, pp. 269–81

CASTLES, S. and MILLER, M. 2009 *The Age of Migration: International Population Movements in the Modern World*, 4th edn, Basingstoke: Palgrave

CASTLES, S. and VAN HEAR, N. 2005 'The migration-asylum nexus: definitions and dimensions', paper presented at the 9th International Association for the Study of Forced Migration (IASFM) Biennial Conference, São Paulo, Brazil, 9–13 January

CHAVEZ, L. 1994 'The power of the imagined community: the settlement of undocumented Mexicans and Central Americans in the United States', *American Anthropologist*, vol. 96, no. 1, pp. 52–73

CVAJNER, M. and SCIORTINO, G. 2010 'Theorizing irregular migration: the control of spatial mobility in differentiated societies', *European Journal of Social Theory*, vol. 13, no. 3, pp. 389–404

DE GENOVA, N. 2002 'Migrant "illegality" and deportability in everyday life', *Annual Review of Anthropology*, vol. 31, pp. 419–47

GILBERT, A. and KOSER, K. 2006 'Coming to the UK: what do asylum-seekers know about the UK before arrival', *Journal of Ethnic and Migration Studies*, vol. 32, no. 7, pp. 1209–25

GINER, C. 2007 'The politics of childhood and asylum in the UK', *Children and Society*, vol. 21, no. 4, pp. 249–60

GORDON, I., SCANLON, K., TRAVERS, T. and WHITEHEAD, C. 2009 *Economic Impact on London and the UK of an Earned Regularisation of Irregular Migrants in the UK*, Interim Report, London: London School of Economics and Political Sciences

HALL, S. 1992 'The question of cultural identity', in Stuart Hall, David Held and Andrew McGrew (eds), *Modernity and its Futures*, Cambridge: Polity, pp. 274–316

HARVEY, A. 2002 'The 1999 Asylum and Immigration Act and how to challenge it', in Steve Cohen, Beth Humphries and Ed Mynott (eds), *From Immigration Controls to Welfare Controls*, London: Routledge, pp. 187–202

HAVINGA, T. and BÖCKER, A. 1999 'Country of asylum by choice or chance: asylum-seekers in Belgium, the Netherlands and the UK', *Journal of Ethnic and Migration Studies*, vol. 25, no. 1, pp. 43–61

HOME OFFICE 2005 *Sizing the Unauthorised (illegal) Migrant Population in the United Kingdom in 2001*, RDSD, Online Report 29/05, London: Home Office

JORDAN, B. and DÜVELL, F. 2002 *Irregular Migration: The Dilemmas of Transnational Mobility*, Cheltenham: Edward Arnold

KOOPMANS, R. and STATHAM, P. (eds) 2000 *Challenging Immigration and Ethnic Relations Politics: Comparative European Perspectives*, Oxford: Oxford University Press

KOSER, K. 2005 *Irregular Migration, State Security and Human Security*, Geneva: Global Commission on International Migration, http://www.gcim.org/attachements/TP5.pdf

KOSER, K. and PINKERTON, C. 2002 *The Social Networks of Asylum Seekers and the Dissemination of Information about Countries of Asylum*, London: Home Office

MAI, N. 2007 'Errance, migration and male sex work', in Susan Ossman (ed.), *Places We Share: Migration, Subjectivity, and Global Mobility*, Lanham, MD: Lexington Books, pp. 97–119

MARGOLIS, M. 1994 *Little Brazil: An Ethnography of Brazilian Immigrants in New York City*, Princeton, NJ: Princeton University Press

O'CONNELL DAVIDSON, J. and FARROW, C. 2007 *Child Migration and the Construction of Vulnerability*, Sweden: Save the Children

RATTANSI, A. and PHOENIX, A. 2005 'Rethinking youth identities: modernist and postmodernist frameworks', *Identity*, vol. 5, no. 2, pp. 97–123

ROBINSON, V. and SEGROTT, J. 2002 *Understanding the Decision-making of Asylum Seekers*, Home Office Research Study 243, London: Home Office

ROSE, N. 1996 'Identity, genealogy, history', in S. Hall and P. Du Gay (eds), *Questions of Cultural Identity*, London: Sage, pp. 128–50

SALES, R. 2007 *Understanding Immigration and Refugee Policy: Contradictions and Continuities*, Bristol: The Policy Press

SOLOMOS, J. 2003 *Race and Racism in Britain*, 3rd edn, Basingstoke: Palgrave Macmillan

VOLLMER, B. 2008 *Undocumented Migration: Counting the Uncountable: Data and Trends: Country Report: UK*, EU Clandestino Project

WILLEN, S. 2007 'Towards a critical phenomenology of "illegality": state power, criminalisation and abjectivity among undocumented migrant workers in Tel Aviv, Israel', *International Migration*, vol. 45, no. 3, pp. 8–36

WYN, J. and WHITE, R. 1997 *Rethinking Youth*, London, Thousand Oaks, CA, and New Delhi: Sage

ZETTER, R., GRIFFITHS, D., PEARL, M. and FERRETTI, S. 2003 *An Assessment of the Impact of Asylum Policies in Europe 1990–2000*, Research Study 259, London: Home Office

ZIMMERMANN, S. 2009 'Irregular secondary movements to Europe: seeking asylum beyond refuge, and the links between these stages', *Journal of Refugee Studies*, vol. 22, no. 1, pp. 1–23

The uneasy ties of working and belonging: the changing situation for undocumented Zimbabwean migrants in northern South Africa

Blair Rutherford

Abstract

This paper examines some of the mechanisms of inclusion/exclusion operating for Zimbabweans on the commercial farms and in the border town of Musina in northern South Africa since the 2000s. In particular, it looks at the changing political economic and regulatory contexts as well as the particular 'modes of belonging' operating in these two sites. Undocumented and documented Zimbabwean migrants have worked through these changing contexts, becoming included or excluded through overlapping, hierarchical 'modes of belonging' operating at localized scales. Such forms of inclusion/exclusion of variable durability generate senses of (in)security for the Zimbabwean migrants that directly inform their livelihood strategies in South Africa. This paper seeks to shed light on such socio-political nexuses in this border zone and contribute to conceptualizing undocumented workers more broadly.

In late 2008, South African and international media stories began carrying accounts of the growing humanitarian crisis of Zimbabweans waiting for their asylum-seeker permit in an overcrowded site nominally administered by the South African government's Department of Home Affairs in Musina. This small town is located just south of the Limpopo river, which marks the border between South Africa and Zimbabwe. Until the 2000s, Musina rarely made the national South African news let alone becoming the focus of international media. This town periodically flashed across the mass-mediated screens and pages until early March 2009 when the South African government abruptly closed down the Refugee Reception Office (RRO) located in the 'Showground'. Since the last third of 2008, thousands of Zimbabweans had been sleeping in the poorly serviced, unsheltered municipal designated space in the hot sun, often for a number of days, if not weeks, to receive a document that gave them a claim legible to state authorities to remain in South Africa, at least for a few months.

There were two complementary narratives of such stories. One outlined the unending economic crisis and political violence as well as the breakdown in social services and rampant cholera in Zimbabwe that drove so many Zimbabweans to jump the border. The other storyline focused on the xenophobia welcoming Zimbabweans in South Africa, with reference to the attacks on 'foreigners' in many of the South African cities in May 2008 and the limited South African government response to the high numbers of Zimbabweans coming to South Africa other than through mass-deportations of 'illegal migrants'.

What was unremarked upon in the media analysis and most of the NGO documents was that on the farms virtually surrounding Musina and going right up to the Limpopo river there were thousands of other Zimbabweans. Many of these migrants had either been living permanently on the farms for years or had been returning annually to take part in the harvest. Whereas many of them began as undocumented migrants, a number were now working under a government document called corporate permits. Indeed, when my research assistant was interviewing people at the Musina RRO in December 2008, he came across a few Zimbabweans coming from the neighbouring farms who moved around the Showground looking for relatives to possibly bring back to their place to wait for their asylum-seeking permit. These Zimbabwean farm workers had a corporate permit which allowed them to get past the police who were looking for undocumented migrants to deport.

This corporate permit is relatively new and it has worked, at times, interchangeably with farmer-issued documents that authorities in the border zone at times recognize as legitimate claims of belonging. Moreover, there were more changes during my trip to Musina in June 2009 in the regulatory field for Zimbabweans who jump the border.

How does one understand this complex spatial terrain, the shifting regulations, and diverse and changing possibilities for Zimbabwean migrants in northern South Africa which provided different possibilities for them depending on where they were? And what does this specific example tell us about understanding undocumented migration more broadly?

There are different analytical tactics taken in the academic literature to understand undocumented migrants. One stream focuses on the migrants themselves, their aspirations, livelihoods, and everyday tactics, including transnational ones, often in the face of various forms of insecurity (e.g., Chavez 1998; Grzymala-Kazlowska 2005). Whereas these more ethnographic studies provide rich insight into the networks, strategies of livelihoods and belonging, and conflicts involving such migrants, the wider political economy shaping laws and policies that define and regulate undocumented migrants can fall outside their scope. Such phenomena do come into view in a literature that examines regulatory frameworks, laws and policy development – what at times is called the wider 'immigration regime' (e.g., Jenson 2007) – in regards to undocumented migrants (e.g., De Genova 2002; Schuster and Solomos 2002; Walters 2006). Often drawing on political economy and governmentality literatures, these studies provide rich insight into the national scale regulations over undocumented migrants and their implications for sovereignty, labour exploitation, citizenship, and inclusion and exclusion within states.

In this paper, I draw on the conceptual focus on regulation found in the latter literature but I use it to understand how it is modulated by particular socio-political dynamics in this South African border zone. In so doing, I supplement this political economy/governmentality literature that tends to concentrate on the national scale or showing how national laws and regulations shape local contexts. I argue instead that forms of authority in sub-national locations can shape national regulations as much as the other way around. National laws and policies matter, but if one solely focuses on them one can miss out the particular play of spatial politics that shape the livelihoods and forms of security/insecurity of undocumented immigrants.

I thus focus on the more localized scale like the ethnographic literature. However, the emphasis here will be more on the dynamic and spatialized regulatory contexts rather than on the everyday lives and tactics of the undocumented migrants. The key concept I use to do the work to provide this focus on localized regulation is 'mode of belonging', a term that is resonant in the literature on citizenship in Africa (e.g., Nyamnjoh 2006; Geschiere 2009). These authors have noted a growing concern with 'belonging' in Africa as they focus on the subtle and emotive processes of distinguishing claims to a locale between 'insiders' and 'outsiders', political processes that are 'often less a defense of the local than efforts to exclude others from access to the new circuits of riches and power' (Gesciehre 2009, p. 26). In this paper, the concept mode of belonging is used to examine the relations through which people, including undocumented migrants, can make claims to reside in, and possibly access means of livelihood, in different spaces.

The ability to stake claims to belong to a territory of any scale rests, in part, on how one is incorporated into the site through reigning practices of power and authority (Lund 2008). These can include an array of state and non-state actors which play a crucial role in everyday processes that forge the criteria of belonging within a territory and a population and through which people, including undocumented migrants, can make some sort of claims of belonging (e.g., Ong 1996). Modes of belonging are the routinized discourses, social practices, and institutional arrangements through which people make claims for recognition and rights, the ways through which they become 'incorporated' or not within the social fabric of everyday life in particular sites (Rutherford 2008). These modes of belonging entail particular figures of authority, those who are able to help constitute who belongs and in what way to particular sites, and particular criteria of belonging that are often gendered, classed, raced, and may be tied to citizenship and forms of nationality. Although modes of belonging may generate criteria and enforcement of belonging in a very specific locality, they are always entangled in translocal processes.

To understand how some locations provide differential forms of security and insecurity to Zimbabweans, with or without documentation, I will examine the wider political economic contexts and international and national policy, legal and political processes shaping human mobility and immigration, as well as the particular 'modes of belonging' operating in these sites.

Such forms of inclusion/exclusion of variable durability generate senses of security and insecurity for Zimbabwean migrants that directly inform their livelihood strategies in South Africa. In short, particular South African spaces have differential forms of (in)security for those variously marked as Zimbabwean, depending on the mechanisms of inclusion/exclusion operating in those spaces and the regulatory and socio-political dynamics occurring at the time.

From this conceptual angle, laws and policies at the national scale, although powerful and influential, are enforced and implemented differently in varied locations as they become entangled through differential authorities operating in overlapping spaces. Governmental interventions are of consequence, but how they actually play out in terms of affecting the migrants and their livelihood possibilities depends on how they become entangled with pre-existing forms of inclusion/exclusion.

I examine two key spaces for Zimbabwean migrants in northern South Africa: the commercial farms and humanitarian sites within the town of Musina. These spaces are the locations in which most Zimbabweans in the region have resided since 2000 (more than the former Bantustans, national parks, and mines). The main focus is on the mechanisms of inclusion/exclusion operating at the level of the sites themselves *vis-à-vis* state authorities, with just a cursory look at the workings of membership criteria and authority and the entailing subjectivities operating for Zimbabweans within these sites. I start by briefly discussing my methodology and then provide some of the wider political, economic, and regulatory contexts before examining particular modes of belonging themselves.

Methods

Since 2004, I have returned to Musina and the surrounding area during their winter months every year but one, for varied lengths of time. Until 2006, I focused solely on Zimbabwean farm workers and carried out ethnographic research on a few commercial farms, and conducted interviews with a number of Zimbabwean farm workers, South African commercial farmers, as well as with officials in NGOs and South African governmental bodies. In 2008 and 2009, I began to focus on Zimbabweans in Musina and carried out a series of interviews with different Zimbabweans who arrived in South Africa after 1999 as well as another set of governmental, NGO, and international agency officials. The number of national and international agencies that have a focus on Zimbabwean migrants (as well as the number of researchers) operating in Musina between 2004 and 2009 has more than tripled, demonstrating the growing interest in Zimbabweans in northern South Africa. I also employed a Zimbabwean research assistant who conducted interviews with Zimbabwean migrants on the farms and in Musina for me in December 2008 and in July 2009.

The main topics covered in our interviews with the Zimbabweans include the Zimbabwean's migration history, immigration status and forms of insecurity associated with it, livelihood strategies (in terms of the arrangements involved in how they find food as well as earn income), living conditions, and working conditions. For farmers and officials with NGOs, I asked about their involvement with Zimbabwean migrants, including their role in gaining some sort of status for them in South Africa. I also queried their relationships with other organizations and security forces.

Sampling followed the snowball method, conditioned by the willingness of the person to speak with me or my assistant. Some declined participation due to apprehension of our motives (e.g., they assumed we had political or legal motives) or because they lacked time. A methodological weakness was the limited time spent in participant-observation, examining the Zimbabweans' engagement with others on the farms or in Musina. This limit was due to time constraints on the part of the researchers.

Political, economic, and regulatory contexts

More and more Zimbabweans started to jump the border into South Africa in the late 1990s, driven largely by fast-growing economic inequalities in the structural-adjustment policies in Zimbabwe and attracted by possibilities of making more money in the post-apartheid economy (Crush 1998). After 2000, the numbers increased dramatically. This rapid rise in numbers is directly related to the Zimbabwean African National Union [Patriotic Front] (ZANU [PF]) state-led politicized violence targeting known and suspected Movement for Democratic Change (MDC) supporters and leaders, especially during electoral contests and its forcible and often compulsory acquisition and redistribution of economic resources such as commercial farming land.

Political violence and the politically-induced economic catastrophe are the main reasons why so many Zimbabweans have fled their country (e.g., McGregor and Primorac 2010). South Africa has been the major destination for Zimbabweans, especially through undocumented means (Crush and Tevera 2010).

Until 2009, the general administrative response of South African authorities to this growing number of Zimbabweans was to arrest and deport those without documentation. Very few Zimbabweans who sought refugee status were successful with their application (Polzer 2008). Instead, most Zimbabweans lived the life of undocumented workers, earning a livelihood highly vulnerable to labour abuses and to being caught and deported.

More undocumented Zimbabweans entering South Africa led to a corresponding increase in their deportations. In 2001 there were 17,000 Zimbabweans deported from South Africa in the entire year. In 2007, there were 18,000 Zimbabweans deported in the month of July (HRW 2008; see also Polzer 2009). The scale of deportations increased costs for South African authorities while having no noticeable effect in stopping the movement of Zimbabweans over the border. In turn, more and more activists, national and international NGOs and, by 2008, UN agencies criticized the response of the South African government towards the Zimbabweans in the country and noted the vulnerable conditions many were in because of their undocumented status (Bloch 2008). In turn, xenophobic claims increased in many South African communities. These claims came to national and international mass-mediated prominence with the widespread attacks on 'foreigners' in May 2008 (Hassim, Kupe and Worby 2009).

The growing pressure from civic activists and UN agencies led to the opening, in July 2008, of a Department of Home Affairs Refugee Reception Office in Musina. This RRO enables Zimbabweans and other nationalities looking for refuge to apply for asylum-seeking status just beyond the international border rather than risking the over 400 kilometre trek to Pretoria which previously had been the closest RRO to South Africa's northern border. With the asylum-seeker permit one has legal status in South Africa to travel around until one attends a refugee determination hearing with a Refugee Status Determination Officer who should decide within three months whether one is recognized as a refugee or not in South Africa.

The number of applicants to the Musina RRO increased dramatically. No shelter was provided for those seeking the permits and the majority waited in the bare yard of the Showground for days, or longer, to get their permit. Many who ventured outside the Showground were picked up by South African police for being 'illegal immigrants' and deported to Zimbabwe.

The intense media attention on the living conditions and abuse of those waiting for permits increased until the Department of Home Affairs abruptly shut down the RRO at the Showground in Musina in March 2009. However, the national and international NGO and UN agency involvement with recent Zimbabwean migrants in the border town continued, if not increased, in 2009.

The RRO re-opened across the street from the Showground. The difference was that international humanitarian organizations began supporting faith-based organizations to set up temporary transit shelters in Nancefield, the main township of Musina, to house those waiting for their asylum-seeker permit to be processed. There, asylum-seeking Zimbabweans received minimal shelter to sleep under and some food.

Then, on 3 April 2009, a few weeks before the national elections in South Africa, the outgoing Minister of Home Affairs made a surprise announcement. She waived visas for Zimbabweans legally entering South Africa while allowing those with visitor permits to legally work during a period of ninety days. Moreover, she declared a moratorium on deportations of Zimbabweans who were found in South Africa without proper documents. There have been some implementation issues (Polzer 2009), but the announcement signalled a major shift for Zimbabweans in South Africa.

Since the implementation of the Global Political Agreement between ZANU [PF] and the two MDC parties in February 2009, there have been some improvements in the national economy and the human rights situation in Zimbabwe. But large numbers of Zimbabweans continue to go to South Africa. Many of them make their way to the RRO in Musina – either directly or via the police if they are caught without documents. In June 2009, the RRO was processing between 250 and 400 Zimbabweans a day, Monday to Thursday, and some more on Friday.

These political economic contexts and shifts in policy in Zimbabwe and South Africa have strongly shaped the migration patterns and routes of Zimbabweans to South Africa. But to have a better understanding of how these events and legal and regulatory changes affected the strategies of the Zimbabweans migrants, I now turn to look at some of the more localized strategies of inclusion/exclusion that have shaped their lives in South Africa.

Commercial farms: ambivalent forms of (in)security

> We were just walking to work before 7 am when the police came rushing up and those without ID cards went running to the bushes. A few of the women later claimed the police beat them. I didn't have my ID and got picked up. I explained to the police that I had it back in my room [in the farm compound], so I traveled with them as they were going to the other rooms of some of the other workers they picked up, looking for their ID cards. After some time, they just let me go as they said I was "talking well," as I was speaking in their language, Venda.

These rushed thoughts came from a Zimbabwean farm worker I call Garikayi during lunchtime on 16 June 2008, outside an orange pack-shed on a farm hugging the south bank of the Limpopo river in northern Limpopo province, South Africa. Like every other farm in this commercial farming area around Musina the majority of its workers were Zimbabwean. He was talking about an event as routinized in the lives of Zimbabweans working or seeking work on these northern South African farms at that time, as was the soccer tournament that had been held on this same farm the day before, attracting teams of predominantly Zimbabwean farm workers from the nearby South African commercial farms.

Garikayi was elaborating what I had heard the hour before from the white South African farm manager and a neighbouring white farmer. They had been talking about corporate permits, a system introduced in 2005 to enable farmers anywhere in South Africa to legally recruit farm workers from Zimbabwe (HRW 2006, pp. 16–17). These two farmers opined that corporate permits generally worked well in terms of getting Zimbabwean workers. But, they continued, they still had problems with the police and others who enforced immigration laws recognizing that these Zimbabwean farm workers were legal and should not be harassed or deported.

The two farmers illustrated this problem by talking about the police raid on the farms in this border zone that day. The farm manager said the police came early in the morning, intercepting those walking to work from the adjacent compound. They detained Zimbabweans seeking work on the farm as well as Zimbabweans who were working on the farms even if they had IDs. When he realized that the raid had happened, the farm manager had one of his Zimbabwean office clerks print out all the IDs and the corporate permits for his workers and drove to the army camp where those detained were being processed before being deported. As he put it, 'luckily the police superintendent was someone who listened and one could negotiate with and we got them back'.

From the farm manager's perspective, the 'negotiations' entailed reminding the police about the rules they had worked out with farmers in this border zone concerning farm-issued IDs. According to the farmers, workers, and some police officers I met, farmers created and issued IDs to the Zimbabweans they had brought over on corporate permits and made them carry these documents for purposes of identification. The farmers pushed for this rule, for a number were concerned about giving the official immigration documents to the Zimbabwean workers themselves in case, in the words of the neighbouring farmer, 'they leave with these corporate permit documents in the hope of finding work elsewhere'. The farm manager was successful in freeing his workers from the camp.

At times Zimbabweans, like Garikayi, and farmers have room to negotiate with the authorities enforcing immigration rules to be able to stay in South Africa, as they either draw on some demonstration that these particular Zimbabweans belong to South Africa, the farms, or the border zone, or they pay a bribe. Of course, to acquire such a status of getting a corporate permit or a farm ID depends on the complicated dynamics of the particular 'mode of belonging' operating on the farms, the specific concatenation of racialized, ethnicized, and gendered practices along with kin relations, ties to a 'home area', and previous work experience (see e.g., Bolt 2010). I examine here the particular forms of belonging these Zimbabweans can claim on these border farms, the authority of commercial farmers in relation to government authorities, and the changes in recent years.

Until the introduction of corporate permits in 2005, the majority of the farm workers on the farms around Musina were undocumented Zimbabweans. During this time, the farm-issued IDs often worked as a recognizable legitimate document for police, soldiers, and Home Affairs officials who patrolled the border region, even though the Zimbabwean workers who were carrying these farmer-created cards had no legal documents authorizing their presence in South Africa. In the 1990s, this border zone had been a zone of exception for Zimbabwean farm workers, whereby South African immigration authorities used quasi-legal means to enable farmers to recruit

Zimbabweans as farm workers without going through the normal immigration channels (Lincoln and Maririke 2000).

In the early 2000s, the special exemptions ended on the understanding that new arrangements under the revised Immigration Act would legalize the import of these farm workers. In the interim, until the corporate permits began to be offered in 2005, farmers in the border zone were able to unofficially use these farmer-created ID cards as quasi-legal documents in this zone. This privilege was not extended to other parts of Limpopo province. Most of the time, my interviewees told me, farm workers could show these cards when stopped by soldiers, police, or Home Affairs officials in the streets of Musina or if the latter raided the farms looking for 'illegals' as a way to show they 'belonged' to South Africa as workers for these predominantly white farmers. These farmer-issued cards thus often prevented them from being deported, with the public authority of the farmers being viewed as having state-sanction, drawing on the previous hegemonic position white farmers held in the administration of farm workers during apartheid and earlier periods (Jeeves and Crush 1997).

At the time, Zimbabwean farm workers recognized the cards offered them some protection from deportation but not much more. A common theme in my interviews with them was that one 'lacked freedom' on the farm. 'Yes,' Tendai, a permanent Zimbabwean farm worker told me in July 2005, 'with this ID the farmer prevents me from being deported when the soldiers come to the compound. But does it allow me to report abuses or ask for better houses or have relatives remain with me on the farm? The Boss is the only one who makes the rules here.' Working conditions were hard on the farms I visited then and most workers earned lower than minimum wages. The hierarchical, racialized mode of belonging common on commercial farms in the region prevailed (e.g., Rutherford 2001), with the catch being the workers felt even more trapped due to their desperation for some currency and uncertain legal status outside the farms. In 2005, a Zimbabwean farm worker compared his previous experience working on the Triangle sugar estate in Zimbabwe with the South African farm:

> I worked from 1994–2000 on Triangle as a [sugar] cane cutter. I had health problems and returned to my rural home in Zimbabwe, scraping by with subsistence farming. But the drought of 2004 meant I came here this year looking for work. Conditions in the fields here are harder. The foremen use the sjambok (whip) [on us]. Not too often but they carry it. They are very harsh. Farm work is similar to that in Triangle, but no sjamboks in Triangle and there is no washing facilities here and sanitation is worse (see also Rutherford and Addison 2007).

Corporate permits became more widespread by 2006, at least on the farms close to the border. Although the corporate permit is supposed to be issued to Zimbabweans recruited in Zimbabwe, in practice on many farms the Zimbabwean workers began as undocumented migrants in South Africa. Zimbabweans still come looking for work on the farms after jumping the border and then either the farmers seek to include them under their corporate permit by going through a set of international bureaucratic procedures or they employ them as undocumented workers. A number of the Zimbabweans arriving there are not looking for long-term work – they are simply seeking a bit of money to allow them to move further south.

South African security forces commonly carried out raids on many of the farms in 2008 and earlier, looking for 'illegals' and occasionally picking up those Zimbabweans who had corporate permits. As in the example of Garikayi, at times farmers were able to successfully negotiate with the authorities, showing that they were often recognized as legitimate mediators. Moreover, many Zimbabwean farm workers in my study felt more secure with the corporate permit. But, in the words of Dumisami, another farm worker, in June 2008:

> Life here is still uncertain. Yes, I have the corporate permit but in the middle of the night when the soldiers break your door down during a raid, your body shakes, even if they accept your permit as legitimate. And I know others who had their permits ripped up by the soldiers and deported.

This concern was lifted earlier with the moratorium on deportations. The farm workers I met in June 2009 told me that the raids had virtually ceased on the farms. Those with corporate permits said they felt more secure than ever before as they worked to earn South African Rand for their own needs and to help support dependents in Zimbabwe.

In short, commercial farms have provided a form of inclusion for Zimbabweans in South Africa to earn a livelihood, albeit a low-paying and possibly harsh one. Their inclusion is contingent on the mode of belonging and its forms of authority of the largely white commercial farmers in the implementation of administrative regulation of the immigration regime. Their ability to stay and work, to being 'incorporated', is directly linked to the decisions and actions of the management of the farm. Such a mode of belonging has provided some security since 2000 in terms of protection from deportation, but it has been highly ambivalent as it has depended on their ability to endure the work regime and depends on their relationship with management and, at times, the ability of the white farmers to negotiate with different state authorities.

Musina: humanitarian zones as modes of belonging

The modes of belonging in Musina are more diffuse and are as informed by changing regulations and circumstances. These affect the space of the town itself as well as more intra-town sites. My research here is ongoing, so I will focus mainly on the varied uses of humanitarian spaces as a particular mode of belonging by some Zimbabwean migrants.

In June 2008, before the RRO was opened, Musina was like a holding pen for Zimbabweans. At that time, the police and Home Affairs officials did not frequently raid known locations where recently arrived Zimbabweans were living or going to within the town. At that point, many Zimbabweans resided in either the houses being built by the state in Nancefield or in a few of the small forested places near the town. Many also made their way to church-run feeding centres for small care packages and food they organized for undocumented Zimbabweans. There were constant police road blocks all around Musina, picking up undocumented Zimbabweans travelling along the roads, particularly those heading south to the major South African urban centres. The Zimbabweans I met in Musina interpreted this as a way to prevent a 'flood' further south, as more and more Zimbabweans were jumping the border as political violence against perceived MDC supporters had dramatically increased after the elections in late March with the run-up to the presidential run-off election scheduled to occur at the end of June.

For example, I met Tapera at a food drop organized by the Catholic Church in one of the townships. He had worked for the previous eight years at a farm supply store in Harare and smaller towns in Zimbabwe. He said as he had not been paid for several months he had decided to jump the border to find money to feed his children. He and a dozen other young men were living in the bushes outside this township, near a stream where they washed their clothes. Some of the young men he lived with told me about escaping from ZANU [PF] forcible recruitment into youth gangs to terrorize suspected MDC members. These young men took odd jobs from the township residents such as cutting wood for a day in exchange for some food. Others, Tapera continued, 'are brought to the old copper mine [in the centre of Musina] during the night by men where they are given shovels and picks to dig for iron cast off from the old mine. They give whatever old iron they find for the night's work to the men in exchange for half a loaf of bread and a freezit [sugared water in a plastic slip]'. Tapera noted that they sleep together for protection – as 'the people who live here, including Zimbabweans who came some years before, look down upon us' – but they were able to move in certain parts of Musina without harassment from the police such as the spot where they received weekly food packages from the Catholic Church.

Shortly after that period, circumstances in terms of spaces of security and insecurity shifted significantly when the Home Affairs opened up the RRO in Musina in July and other international and national organizations began to station permanent officers in town.

My research assistant visited the RRO at the Showground in December 2008 and found varied forms of security and insecurity for different Zimbabweans. Those who made it to the Showground were able to get access to permits, sometimes after a long wait or, as a number interviewees attested, through bribery. According to NGO officials interviewed in 2009, the aim had been to keep the undocumented migrants in the space around the RRO until they received their asylum-seeker permit. But many Zimbabweans were wary of leaving that space without permits as they could be picked up and deported.

For instance, a Zimbabwean who was selling furniture for his Zimbabwean-based employer at an intersection near the Showground told my research assistant in December 2008, 'the police come every day and park their cars here.... They put up their roadblock here arresting people coming from the Showground without the asylum permits or visa'. The furniture seller himself did not have a permit and slept next to his wares at night but confided to my assistant that the police did not bother him, musing 'I think my employer has a connection with the police here because I am not harassed'.

The Showground became not only a place to get one's permit but it became a permissible ground to stay while the Zimbabweans sought their next moves. For instance, my research assistant met a Zimbabwean man and his younger brother who had received their asylum-seeker permit a few weeks earlier after a week's wait. But they were still living in the Showground with other relatives, trying to raise money to send back to Zimbabwe to bring more of their family members to Musina to get their permits. They engaged in a series of part-time jobs. Their hope was to get enough money to bring other siblings to Musina and then once everyone had asylum-seeker permits, to raise enough money to travel to Johannesburg to look for 'real jobs'. But stepping outside the Showground at that time was a risk. As one commented, when unloading trucks they had to return in the early evening and often 'we meet the police who then arrest us saying we are not supposed to walk at night. They take us to the police station where they detain us and release us the following morning'. At that time, humanitarian spaces proved to be islands of security in a wider town of insecurity.

Although by June 2009 the Showground was closed, I found the transit shelters and feeding depots run by faith-based organizations could also serve as a base for Zimbabweans to seek livelihoods. International donors, local and national authorities, and NGOs negotiated rules concerning the establishment and running of these temporary shelters, including setting a maximum number of days for Zimbabweans to remain at each specific shelter. The vast majority of people staying in the transit shelters remained until they received their permit and then, as they were supposed to, they moved elsewhere, looking for work. But some established relations with the church authorities running the shelters and resided there for some time as they looked for work or saved money. They acted as a mode of belonging, even if transitory, for some Zimbabweans to use as part of their livelihood strategies. In other words, they became spaces through which they could stake a claim which they could use to seek to generate some resources. These migrant Zimbabweans could attach themselves to the dependencies found in these shelters for their livelihood strategies. For example, one man stayed in one shelter for three months, instead of the three days the regulations governing the shelters declared to be the maximum stay. He sent most of the money he earned from his first contract as an assistant builder to his relatives back in Zimbabwe for, he reasoned, 'I get free food and I have free accommodation at the moment so I do not have much use of the money compared to my family remaining in Zimbabwe'. He was able to do this as he became a dependent of one of the shelter administrators, helping him do work around the space and helping to enforce order in the camp.

Others used the humanitarian places as sites to find jobs. These were done through the hierarchies within the sites themselves. For instance, when I was visiting one transit shelter a black commercial farmer was also there picking up a woman who had been staying there to be his domestic servant. He arranged this through the pastor who helped to run the shelter. In turn, one of the feeding stations in Musina run by a church was well-known as a place to find work in one of the businesses of the church-members who ran it or of those of others who used the site, with the church authorities' permission, to recruit workers.

For example, my research assistant was at this site in July 2009 when a black South African woman arrived in a truck just after the free lunch was served. She talked with the authorities of the feeding site for a few minutes before making her way to the group of largely Zimbabwean men eating. She said she wanted nine men to clear some land for her and asked for groups of three men to bid on each piece to clear. A short bidding war ensued and she took the lowest bidders in her truck.

The government recognition of the asylum-seeker permit and the moratorium on deportation provided some relief for many Zimbabweans in Musina. Like the commercial farms, the sites of humanitarianism such as transit camps or feeding centres in late 2008 and 2009 provided some forms of security *vis-à-vis* immigration authorities as well as bases from which to secure some livelihoods, albeit often precarious and temporary ones. Zimbabweans were able to use these sites to try to avoid deportation before the 2009 moratorium was issued as well as to draw on ties to the authorities within these spaces for employment opportunities. The 2009 changes in immigration regulations concerning Zimbabweans opened up new spaces for many in Musina to openly navigate. Yet, many continued to draw on the particular modes of belonging and authority operating in the humanitarian spaces as they sought a livelihood, minimal and fragile as it often was.

Conclusion

By examining how the specific sites of commercial farms and humanitarian spaces in Musina in northern South Africa have modulated national-scale regulations concerning undocumented immigrants, this paper seeks to illustrate an analytical strategy that supplements that wider political economy/governmentality literature by attending to specific contours of authority in particular sites. Discussing how Zimbabweans from 2005–2009 worked through particular modes of belonging operating in these sites in relationship to wider scale regulations and laws provides ethnographic insight into the complex spatial terrain of regulations governing undocumented migrants.

The wider immigration regime has strongly influenced the ability of Zimbabweans to find documents that are legible to state authorities, enabling them to claim a form of belonging in South Africa. The laws and regulations shape the ability of Zimbabweans to secure different types of livelihoods. By tracing how this regime becomes entangled in particular modes of belonging and their forms of authority, however, one is able to understand how the latter can assume state-like powers or act as a mediator and facilitator for these Zimbabweans to acquire documents that are recognizable by state authorities and more easily enable them to access varied forms of livelihoods.

This paper thus provides insight into the particular forms of inclusion and exclusion operating for Zimbabweans in northern South Africa in the first decade of the twenty-first century. It not only shows how laws and regulations excluded Zimbabweans who were undocumented – touching on the dominant theme of the literature on 'belonging' in Africa that analyses the 'growing importance of identity politics and more exclusionary ideas of citizenship' (Nyamnjoh 2006, p. 3) the sharpening divisions between 'insiders' and 'outsiders' – but it also analyses how some of these same Zimbabweans could find forms of inclusion through the authority figures in modes of belonging operating on commercial farms and, in Musina, humanitarian spaces in this border zone. Such forms of inclusion were often tied with livelihoods – explicitly so on the commercial farms and perhaps surprisingly so in the humanitarian spaces. These forms of inclusion could be exploitative and very precarious, but given the unfolding economic and political crises in Zimbabwe, many Zimbabweans explained to me that they had to pursue such uneasy ties of working and belonging at this moment in time.

References

BLOCH, ALICE 2008 'Gaps in protection: undocumented Zimbabwean migrants in South Africa', *Forced Migration Studies Programme Working Paper No. 38*, Johannesburg: University of Witwatersrand Press

BOLT, MAXIM 2010 'Camaraderie and its discontents: class consciousness, ethnicity and divergent masculinities among Zimbabwean migrant farmworkers in South Africa', *Journal of Southern African Studies*, vol. 36, no. 2, pp. 377–93

CRUSH, JONATHAN (ed.) 1998 *Beyond Control: Immigration & Human Rights in a Democratic South Africa*, Kingston, ON: Southern African Migration Project

CRUSH, JONATHAN and DANIEL TEVERA (eds) 2010 *Zimbabwe's Exodus: Crisis, Migration, Survival*, Kingston: Southern African Migration Program

CHAVEZ, LEO 1998 *Shadowed Lives: Undocumented Immigrants in American Society*, 2nd edn, Toronto: Harcourt Brace College Publishers

DE GENOVA, NICHOLAS 2002 'Migrant "illegality" and deportability in everyday life', *Annual Review of Anthropology*, vol. 31, pp. 419–47

GESCHIERE, PETER 2009 *The Perils of Belonging: Autochthony, Citizenship, and Exclusion in Africa & Europe*, Chicago: University of Chicago Press

GRZYMALA-KAZLOWSKA, ALEXSANDRA 2005 'From ethnic cooperation to in-group competition: undocumented Polish workers in Brussels', *Journal of Ethnic and Migration Studies*, vol. 31, no. 4, pp. 675–97

HASSIM, SHIREEN, TAWANA, KUPE and ERIC, WORBY 2009 *Go Home or Die Here: Violence, Xenophobia and the Reinvention of Difference in South Africa*, Johannesburg: University of Witwatersrand Press

HUMAN RIGHTS WATCH [HRW] 2006 *Unprotected Migrants: Zimbabweans in South Africa's Limpopo Province*, New York: HRW

HUMAN RIGHTS WATCH [HRW] 2008 *Neighbors in Need: Zimbabweans Seeking Refuge in South Africa*, New York: HRW

JENSON, JANE 2007 'The European Union's citizenship regime. Creating norms and building practices', *Comparative European Politics*, vol. 5, no. 1, pp. 53–69

JEEVES, ALAN and JONATHAN CRUSH (eds) 1997 *White Farms, Black Labor: The State and Agrarian Change in Southern Africa, 1910–1950*, Portsmouth, NH: Heinemann

LINCOLN, DAVID and CLAUDE, MARIRIKE 2000 'Southward migrants in the far north: Zimbabwean farmworkers in Northern Province', in Crush Jonathan (ed.), *Borderline Farming: Foreign Migrants in South African Commercial Agriculture*, Kingston: South African Migration Project, pp. 40–62

LUND, CHRISTIAN 2008 *Local Politics and the Dynamics of Property in Africa*, Cambridge: Cambridge University Press

MCGREGOR, JOANN and RANKA PRIMORAC (eds) 2010 *Zimbabwe's New Diaspora: Displacement and the Cultural Politics of Survival*, Oxford: Berghahn

NYAMNJOH, FRANCIS 2006 *Insiders & Outsiders: Citizenship and Xenophobia in Contemporary Southern Africa*, London: Zed Books

ONG, AIHWA 1996 'Cultural citizenship as subject-making: new immigrants negotiate racial and ethnic boundaries', *Current Anthropology*, vol. 37, no. 5, pp. 737–62

POLZER, TARA 2008 'South African government and civil society responses to Zimbabwean migration', *Southern African Migration Program Policy Brief No. 22*, Kingston: Southern African Migration Project

POLZER, TARA 2009 'Regularising Zimbabwean migration to South Africa', *Migration Policy Brief*, May. Johannesburg: Consortium for Refugees and Migrants in South Africa and University of Witwatersrand's Forced Migration Studies Programme

RUTHERFORD, BLAIR 2001 *Working on the Margins: White Farmers, Black Workers in Postcolonial Zimbabwe*, London: Zed

RUTHERFORD, BLAIR 2008 'Conditional belonging: farm workers and the cultural politics of recognition in Zimbabwe', *Development and Change*, vol. 39, no. 1, pp. 73–99

RUTHERFORD, BLAIR and LINCOLN, ADDISON 2007 'Zimbabwean farm workers in northern South Africa', *Review of African Political Economy*, vol. 34, no. 114, pp. 619–35

SCHUSTER, LIZA and JOHN, SOLOMOS 2002 'Rights and wrongs across European borders: migrants, minorities and citizenship', *Citizenship Studies*, vol. 6, no. 1, pp. 37–54

WALTERS, WILLIAM 2006 "Border/control', *European Journal of Social Theory*, vol. 9, no. 2, pp. 187–204

Navigating the US-Mexico border: the crossing strategies of undocumented workers in Tijuana, Mexico

Sergio Chávez

Abstract

What strategies do undocumented workers employ to cross the US-Mexico border? And how does the implementation of border enforcement affect crossing strategies? Drawing on ethnographic research, I compare the border crossing patterns of undocumented and documented migrants in Tijuana who cross the border to work without authorization in the US. My findings suggest that, prior to border enforcement, crossers entered informally and without documentation. In some instances, these undocumented workers crossed the border alone or relied on local smugglers to avoid detection. In other instances, undocumented crossers gained entry by declaring their connections to US employers. Now, border enforcement has drastically reduced undocumented crossings through Tijuana. In this new era, the primary way to obtain undocumented work is by acquiring a Border Crossing Card that allows a migrant to cross (but not work) legally. This group of Mexican migrants are now authorized to cross the border but not to work in the US, and so it is imperative to conceal all evidence of their labours from port officials.

> Many people say that it is luck to be able to cross the border everyday, but it depends on who you get [state official] to be able to get lucky... Viviana Ramos, daily border crosser.

Introduction

Operation Gatekeeper was instituted at the Tijuana-San Diego border sector in 1994 to curtail the flow of clandestine crossings. Gatekeeper was part of a United States campaign known as 'Prevention through Deterrence'. Its purpose was to reduce clandestine border crossings in heavily-transited points such as El Paso, Texas, and San Diego, California. As an immigration law enforcement strategy, Gatekeeper increased the number of patrol agents, introduced sophisticated surveillance technology, and increased the miles of iron fence separating Mexico from the US. Before Gatekeeper, 50 per cent of undocumented Mexican migrants crossed through Tijuana; 98 per cent of California-bound migrants crossed the border here (Bustamante 1990, p. 215; Massey, Durand and Malone 2002, p. 108). Gatekeeper's new enforcement tactics transformed how and where migrants entered the US.

This study compares the border crossing practices of undocumented and documented border crossers before and after border enforcement was introduced in the Tijuana-San Diego sector. I focus on these two groups to examine the variety of strategies that migrants use to cross international borders to gain access to undocumented work, arguing that each group uses different strategies. These strategies are historically specific and reflective of the border policies that govern international travel. I suggest that these crossing strategies are also based on the opportunities available to migrants.

First, a distinction: by *undocumented crossers*, I refer to two groups of people who crossed the border by evading inspection at the US port of entry prior to the escalation of border enforcement in 1994. This includes *transient undocumented crossers* who used Tijuana as a point of entry for interior US labour markets as well as *daily undocumented crossers* who circulated on a daily basis to access regional agricultural markets along the US-Mexico boundary. By *documented crossers*, I refer to those who use Border Crossing Cards (BCCs) to seek out unauthorized US employment during an era of border enforcement. A BCC, issued by the US consular offices in Mexico, entitles the bearer to enter the US for a period of seventy two hours within a twenty-five-mile radius solely for tourism, shopping, and social visits, but does not allow for employment on either a temporary or long-term basis.

To date, most studies on border enforcement have focused on how policies have rerouted migration and crossing patterns for long-distance, undocumented crossers (Singer and Massey 1998; Andreas 2000; Cornelius 2005; Donato et al. 2008; Spener 2009). These studies, however, have not addressed the experiences of people who live in Mexico but cross the border each day to work in the US. Recent studies suggest that migration patterns to and from border cities operate under distinct principles because residents have access to formal channels for entering the US (Herzog 1995; Alegría 2002; Fussell 2004). As such, I focus specifically on the border crossing experience of migrants as they attempt to navigate their entry into the US, and I address three questions: first, what strategies do undocumented workers employ to cross the US-Mexico border? Second, how does the implementation of border enforcement affect crossing strategies? Finally, how does access to legal documents alter the mode of crossing and strategies used?

Review of the literature

Because migration is a costly and risky behaviour, potential migrants use a variety of strategies to ensure safe passage. Migrants typically draw on the social support of family and friends to provide assistance ranging from paying a smuggler to finding work and housing once they arrive in the US (Mines 1981; Massey et al. 1987; Durand, Massey and Zenteno 2001). When migrants do not have a social structure that supports international migration, some studies suggest they engage in a 'step-migration' that consists of moving to another state to obtain assistance from other migrants, employers, and smugglers who are lacking in their communities of origin (Young 1994; Zabin and Hughes 1995; Fussell 2004). One shortcoming of these migration studies is that they limit their analysis to how migrants use resources at either the point of origin or destination, never looking at the actual border crossing experience.

Border enforcement studies, however, provide clues about the strategies migrants use as they cross international borders. Singer and Massey (1998), for instance, have found that migrants relied on family or smugglers to cross during their first trip; as migrants gained experience, they depended less on the assistance of others. More recent studies suggest that escalated border enforcement had led to a shift in how and where migrants cross the border (Eschbach et al. 1999; Andreas 2000; Cornelius 2005). One change is a rerouting of patterns away from San Diego and El Paso's urban areas to crossings in the Sonoran desert. Because these territories are relatively unknown, migrants must now rely on professional smugglers to guide them across (Andreas 2000; Cornelius 2005; Donato et al. 2008; Spener 2009). Taken together, these studies suggest that as border enforcement shifts crossings to the desert, the border crossing experience of previous migrants has become outdated. Further, while these studies suggest previous border crossing experience lowers the odds of apprehension, they do not elaborate on how entry is facilitated by different social actors; the undocumented border crossing experience is treated as static and uniform process. As a result, Spener (2009) suggests that clandestine crossings should be studied as a *process* which takes into consideration all social actors involved and sees the strategies employed by the smugglers and smuggled as constantly changing.

Understanding the border crossing experience as an evolving process is important in border communities. A growing number of scholars have identified the distinct strategies used by BCC holders who cross to work without authorization in the US (Bean et al. 1994; Fussell 2004; Hernández-León 2008). Rubén Hernández-León (2008) examines the interactions between border patrol agents and migrants and outlines how immigration authorities attempt to uncover BCC violators. Heyman (2001, 2002, 2009) looks at the same relationship, studying how immigration officials use ethnicity and class to either grant or deny entry. For example, 'Mexican-looking' individuals are more likely to be harassed and viewed with suspicion when compared to whites and African Americans. Similarly, working-class BCC holders are more likely to be presumed violators when compared to upper-class Mexicans. Although these studies highlight the experience of BCC holders, they focus on the *perspective* of state agents rather than the crossers. My study builds on migration and border enforcement studies by examining the variety of strategies and resources that border crossers use over time.

Methods

This study draws on approximately two years of ethnographic research in Tijuana, Mexico (from September 2004 to January 2006 with return visits in 2007 and 2009–10). The study sample is based on ninety one in-depth interviews with respondents who had worked in the US as *braceros* (guest workers contracted between 1942 and 1964), undocumented migrants, legal migrants, and/or holders of Border Crossing Cards. The sample includes respondents who crossed the border at Tijuana during different historical periods and using a variety of crossing strategies. In addition, I collected detailed information and rich narratives on the respondents' labour histories, crossing patterns, and network ties, and I obtained employer letters and old photographs to provide context to the fluid nature of crossings. All of the names of migrants and employers that appear in this paper have been changed to protect the confidentiality of participants.

Along with in-depth interviews, I conducted hundreds of informal conversations with taxi drivers, street vendors, smugglers, and merchants who helped facilitate the crossings of migrants across borders. I observed interactions as migrants travelled to and from their places of work, including those that took place in the pedestrian and vehicle lanes at the San Ysidro port of entry. I took extensive notes on who crossed and how, and I crossed the border four to six times per week between 4:00 a.m. and 8:00 a.m., the peak time for travel to work, to understand the experiences of this labour community. I also rode the San Diego Trolley and Mexican buses and taxis to document how people moved from their homes in Mexico to their places of work in the US and how they developed connections with other crossers. Finally, I systematically analysed my field notes and interview transcripts to identify key themes and for consistency and variability across data sources.

I arrived in Tijuana ten years after Gatekeeper. By this time, undocumented crossings were almost non-existent – at least compared to previous eras, in which undocumented crossings were the norm (Chavez 1992; Andreas 2000). My findings, then, should not be taken to mean that documented border crossings did not exist before border enforcement or that undocumented crossings never happened afterward. Rather, I suggest that border enforcement during each historical period shapes migrant border crossing strategies and behaviours. Although in 1994 the US government intensified border enforcement in Tijuana-San Diego, people still cross without documents (only now these groups are more often channelled through the Sonoran desert). Today, the most common access to unauthorized US employment through Tijuana is found in navigating formal channels. In the next section, I provide a brief description of the evolution of border enforcement policies, describing the shift from undocumented to documented crossings.

The Escalation of border enforcement

The Immigration Reform and Control Act (IRCA) of 1986 marked a major shift in the way the US government handled undocumented migration. First, it legalized the status of almost three million formerly undocumented immigrants. Next, it created sanctions for firms who hired undocumented workers. Finally, IRCA expanded the Border Patrol staff. Although the legislation was intended to stop undocumented migration, IRCA's success was limited because it focused on the border and not the workplace. IRCA ironically *generated* waves of undocumented migration as return migrants told their friends and relatives about the plethora of jobs available to them in the US (Cornelius 1989; Andreas 2000; Massey, Durand and Malone 2002). Tijuana became a popular crossing point because, even with increased border enforcement, migrants still had a one in three chance of crossing successfully (Singer and Massey 1998). The still relatively lax border enforcement and high probability of crossing after repeated attempts led to massive groups of undocumented migrants congregating in Tijuana (Chavez 1992; Andreas 2000; Nevins 2002).

To gain control of the border and stop the flow of undocumented immigrants that IRCA had created, the US government instituted

Operation Gatekeeper in 1994. Within four years of Gatekeeper's implementation, the number of patrol agents was increased from 980 to 2,264, the miles of fencing expanded from nineteen to forty five miles, and the number of underground sensors grew from 448 to 1,214. Two years after Operation Gatekeeper, the Illegal Immigration Reform and Immigrant Responsibility Act of 1996 led to further levels of increased surveillance. While one border patrol officer was responsible for 1.1 miles of border in 1975, there was one guard for every 1,000 feet by 2004 (Gathman 2008). Andreas (2000, p. 14) asserts that border enforcement made crossings in Tijuana 'less visible and more dispersed' and created an '*image* of a more secure and orderly border' (my emphasis). In the following section, I chronicle the transition from an 'open' to a 'closed' border society and discuss the shift from undocumented to documented crossings.

Open border era: undocumented border crossers

During the 'open border era', there were two groups of undocumented crossers in Tijuana, and each employed distinct crossing strategies. First, transient undocumented crossers either crossed without anyone's assistance or used local smugglers for crossing the international border. After arriving in Tijuana, this group moved on to interior labour markets either within a few hours or a couple of days at most. Daily undocumented crossers, on the other hand, relied on their connections to US employers to enter freely. For daily crossers, declaring their occupational status as agricultural workers and asserting their ties to US employers gave them a pass to the regional agricultural labour market. Despite these differences, both groups shared in their circumventing of inspection and their largely informal mode of entry. Illustrating these experiences, I catalogued the three types of border crossing strategies in the open era.

Self-smuggling

One strategy that transient undocumented migrants used was travelling with friends and family members who helped guide them across the border. Because these crossers, people like Rafael, knew the border terrain (or at least had experienced help), they did not hire smugglers. Rafael first came to the US in 1963 as a guest worker, and he continued crossing clandestinely through Tijuana until the mid-1970s. On his first journey, Rafael left his hometown in the state of Michoacán with his brother and several friends. They arrived at the bus terminal and, from there, took a taxi to the isolated Canyon Zapata (a popular entry point). Once night came, Rafael and his friends ran through the canyons and ravines until they reached San

Ysidro, California. He remembers, 'the first time I came to Tijuana in 1974 it was really easy. I was the type of person who did not need anyone [smugglers] to help me cross. I crossed with other people and we were told to simply cross the line and wait in San Ysidro, California for someone to pick us up.' Rafael crossed the border with ease because the border patrol was almost non-existent at the time. Moreover, he journeyed with friends who provided him with money to pay his bus ticket and then guided him across the international border. Once in the US, they were picked up by another group of friends who drove them to Washington State where they picked apples.

All of the undocumented crossers in my study originally left Mexico because they had a difficult time finding steady jobs. Generally, they received subsistence wages and/or surplus goods from the harvest when they worked in Mexico. Therefore, undocumented crossers did not have money to pay smugglers, depending instead on experienced migrants to guide them across the border. In 1980, Chuy Valentino crossed through Tijuana bound for Los Angeles. Like Rafael, Chuy and his friend crossed through Canyon Zapata without a smuggler. They crossed alone because they did not have money, but also because they wanted to prove to others that it was possible to cross without a smuggler. For years, Chuy and his friend repeated the trip, crossing without assistance sometimes walking all the way to Los Angeles (about 130 miles). During their treks, they mapped safe walking routes and developed detours to safely cross the secondary inspection at the San Clemente, California checkpoint. The poorly-guarded border meant that the odds of successfully crossing were high, especially if migrants relied on experienced friends and family members who knew entry routes. However, when undocumented crossers did not know the route, they had to hire local smugglers to help guide them safely to the US.

Using local smugglers

In 2004, I met Fidel Ramos. At one time, Fidel had helped guide people across the international border. As a guide, he sometimes charged people $10 dollars, while other times he let migrants name their own price for his instruction on how to jump the international fence and in which direction they should run. The services of local guides like Fidel were purchased by undocumented migrants because the guides could tell where the border patrol waited to catch undocumented crossers. They also knew which border patrol agents monitored the border more closely than others. Fidel and his fellow guides knew the lay of the land and used this knowledge (for a fee) to help undocumented crossers enter successfully even when the border patrol was present. But while they generally provided migrants with instructions and knowledge on how to successfully cross the border, the guides didn't actually accompany the migrants across the border.

After several unsuccessful attempts to cross the border through the remote hills of Tijuana, Hugo Campos hired a local smuggler to help him navigate the border. He recalls how he crossed through Playas de Tijuana (a public beach located along the Pacific Ocean) in the 1980s: 'I crossed by the beach, running – it was really easy. My brother and I crossed pretending to be surfers'. So while some local smugglers' strategies consisted of evading border patrol agents, Hugo's smuggler helped him blend into the local surfer culture of Imperial Beach, California, dressing him as a surfer to confuse the border patrol. Other local guides told me that they dressed their clients in athletic clothes and had them jog right past border patrol agents. In these instances, the undocumented crossers were successful because local guides had carefully studied the international border's weaknesses (including the agents who patrolled it) and passed this knowledge to others. During the open border era, experienced crossers and guides shared knowledge about the best places, times, and ruses to avoid detection and get to the US.

Daily undocumented crossers

While transient undocumented crossers depended on the assistance of family, friends, and local guides to cross, another group of undocumented crossers circulated on a daily basis. This population was comprised primarily of men who had settled with their families in Tijuana to be in close proximity to US farm jobs. Some of these daily undocumented crossers were former *braceros* who had participated in the Bracero Guest Worker Program (1942–1964) between the United States and Mexico. After the programme ended, these men became part of a sort of reserve army of labour that lived in Tijuana, but crossed to work in the US.

Daily undocumented crossers formed part of an 'occupational network' whose unlawful entry was facilitated by their intermediaries, the US-based crop growers who hired them, and labour contractors who sometimes guided them across the border. If stopped by border patrol agents, these migrants simply declared the grower that had hired them. Jesus Márquez, a foreman at one of the local farms, explained that, until the 1980s, a border crosser stopped by border patrol agents might only need to say the name of his employer, 'Edwards and Smith', and he would be allowed to enter the US. Local clandestine crossers were allowed to enter the US labour market, but were reminded by the border patrol to return to Mexico at the end of workday. This relationship was an informal work arrangement between the border patrol and US growers. In this regional labour market, back-and-forth crossings were tolerated as long as migrants filled labour shortages in farms located along the US-Mexico border.

Cresencio López, an eighty-four year old migrant, has recruited workers in the bars and restaurants of Zona Norte and Colonia Libertad. In the 1970s, he received one dollar per person for recruiting men and guiding them to farms in San Diego County. To ensure that these recruits were not confused for transient undocumented crossers and turned away by the border patrol, Cresencio taught his workers how to respond to authorities if stopped *en route* to the farm. He instructed the men to give the name of the employer that had hired them. He also explained to them the type of produce and how it would be tended or harvested should authorities further question their travels to work in the US.

Timothy Dunn (1996, p. 13) suggests that in the American Southwest, the border patrol and growers have long had 'a de facto relationship' defined by the supply and demand of labour. In Tijuana-San Diego, the border patrol often assisted growers by facilitating the entry of workers. Jesus Marquez, the seventy-one year old former *bracero* and labour foreman mentioned previously, remembers: 'back in the time the border patrol would pick you up . . . He would take me to work in Nestor, California. He would give me a ride and leave me there'. Once the border patrol came to know Jesus as a daily crosser with ties to Tijuana, he was allowed to enter the country with his labour crew from Mexico. And Raúl Ramírez, an internal migrant from Michoacán, remembers how his employer threw frequent parties to thank border patrol agents for allowing his Mexican workers to enter the US freely. He explains:

> My boss he used to throw a fiesta [party] every 15 days for the border patrol . . . So when we crossed they asked us, "who do you work with?" and we replied, "Martinez" and they would say "ok, come on in!"

The undocumented crossers' narratives depict a border through which migrants circulated freely on a seasonal or daily basis, depending on whether they were transient workers or daily commuters. During the 'open border era', crossing patterns were largely characterized as informal due to the lack of institutional regulation controlling labour flows and the close ties between employers and border patrol agents. With border enforcement though, undocumented crossing became almost non-existent in Tijuana after 1994. People continue to cross, only now the primary means of entry has become the presentation of legal documents to immigration agents. I now turn to the experiences of these people, documented to travel, but undocumented to work.

Closed border era: documented crossers, undocumented workers

Unlike undocumented crossers who circumvented inspection, documented crossers did not evade state authorities. Instead, they used BCCs to come into the US officially at the port of entry. When I arrived in 2004, ten years of Gatekeeper had effectively stopped undocumented crossings in Tijuana and diverted them to the Sonoran desert. Nonetheless, people continued to cross from Tijuana to the US in a new stream comprised of people using BCCs, ostensibly for visitation, but, in truth, to access undocumented employment. After working in Tijuana to save up money and increase their chances of obtaining a BCC, the migrants used that documentation to cross into the US legally and obtain work illegally.

BCCs as a primary mode of entry

Twenty-one year old Carmen Castro moved from Oaxaca to Tijuana with the intention of crossing without documents. When Carmen arrived, she found a job in a department store and began saving money to hire a well-known smuggler to help her cross the border. During that time, her brother and co-worker applied for and successfully obtained BCCs, which they used to work without authorization in the US. Carmen's brother and friend encouraged her to forego the idea of crossing without documents and instead asked her to continue working full-time and open a bank account. After one year, she applied for a BCC. She explains how her friend coached her:

> A friend helped me through the process of the BCC everything from which paperwork I needed to take. In fact, she got her [BCC] first then encouraged me to apply and helped me with the paperwork. We also went together to our employer to ask for letters [of recommendation for the BCC].

Once she got her card, Carmen and her friend crossed the international border pretending they were going to eat at a San Diego restaurant. They passed inspection, then took a bus to Los Angeles, where Carmen eventually found employment in a food processing factory.

For Tijuana residents, the BCC is a resource. They can use it to enter the US labour market temporarily, as is the case for daily commuters, or on a permanent basis, like Carmen. As border enforcement makes undocumented crossings all but impossible, the BCC has become the primary way to enter the US labour market through Tijuana. However, to cross on a regular basis, documented crossers must convince immigration officials that they are not BCC violators. In the sections that follow, I describe the various strategies used to avoid detection when crossing regularly for unauthorized employment.

The documented border crossing experience

At the US port of entry, an immigration official's job is to stop the flow of contraband (such as drugs) and restrict entry to unauthorized crossers. As a result, immigration officials subjectively assess who they perceive to be in violation of US immigration laws. This subjective approach leads BCC holders to believe that luck matters when crossing the border. Therefore, they are always seeking to increase their chances of success by selecting the correct line and immigration official – these choices can be the difference between being waved through or having a BCC confiscated. Angel García, who began crossing in his early twenties, learned these lessons the hard way. For almost two years, he crossed to work in US construction jobs, but his luck ran out one day and he was suspected of using his BCC to work. Though the US government never proved that he was working in the US, his BCC was revoked. He explains the incident:

> The immigration officer asked me, "Hey, so why are you going so early?" I then told him why. I told him that I was going to pick up my father. He told me, "No you are going to work." He kept telling me and telling me that I was coming to work, and each time, I would say no. He would tell me in English and I would tell him in Spanish. That fucker, must have asked how is it possible that [I] know English . . . He would then tell me things in English and things in Spanish. He tried to force me to tell him that "yes" I was going to work in the US. But I never admitted that. He told me, "That is a privilege . . . a privilege that we give to Mexicans and we take away the privilege when we want to and today your BCC is cancelled." But I asked him, why? For what reason? What rule did I break? The official said, "No, we are just going to cancel it right now!"

Both being granted entry and selected as a suspicious individual were subjective. As Carmen Castro explained, many times this selective enforcement was based on ethnicity.

> I have seen that if a white American passes sometimes they will not even ask them for an ID. Or sometimes they check it really quickly. But if a Latino passes, they will ask you were you are going. How long will you be over there [in the US]? They will ask many

> questions. They will also ask what you have in your purse. Sometimes I carry my small bag and they will ask, "What do you have in the bag?" I say, "Clothes." They will then ask, "Where are you going?"

Although immigration officials attempted to identify violators, they did not always regulate entry for documented crossers. Based on observations and interviews, it seemed that officials were well aware that Tijuana was an important source of labour for San Diego County. During the work rush hour at the port of entry, I saw immigration officials quickly wave crossers through, barely examining their identification cards. One of my informants explained, "The US knows that Tijuana is a working-class barrio for San Diego. They allow it because they get free labour and don't have to provide housing and medical services for transnational workers." While some BCC holders believe that luck matters when crossing the international border, others prefer to control their own odds of apprehension by altering their behaviours.

Masking US occupational identity

To avoid being identified as a violator, BCC holders must convince immigration officials that they are not working in the US. One strategy that respondents identified was mixing modes of entry. For example, people who crossed by car alternated vehicles to prevent immigration officials from documenting a sustained border crossing pattern by tracking their licence plate. These BCC holders borrowed vehicles from friends and family members to confuse immigration officials. Additionally, when possible, BCC holders carpooled with Legal Permanent Residents or US citizens, so immigration officials became distracted by inspecting the vehicle and documents of the driver who had authorization to work in the US. During the check, BCC holders hoped to blend into the background so that immigration officials might forget about their presence.

To further lessen the risk of suspicion, some BCC holders developed plausible stories to hide their real purpose in crossing the border. This method, they hoped, would help avoid extensive questioning about the motives for their travel. And, at all possible costs, BCC holders did not want immigration officials to document their daily crossings either by noting it on the computer or simply registering it on their minds. Cesar Villa, a thirty-three year old BCC holder who works in the shoe department of a US store, explains one strategy he has used.

> I used to carry a lot of documentation of my business and almost always, I say that I am going to see my girlfriend. That way when

> they ask me, "Why do you cross so much?" Well I tell them that I am going to see my girlfriend. And well they then can't ask me anymore questions.

By showing that he had a business in Mexico, Cesar could convince immigration officials that his primary employment ties were in Mexico and not the United States. The documents of business ownership relieved any mistrust that immigration officials had about his daily border crossings, and, by mentioning that he had a girlfriend in the US, Cesar presented a convincing story for why he needed to cross the border so often.

Another story that BCC holders used to hide their US occupational status was telling immigration officials that their primary purpose of crossing was one of consumption. However, research participants learned quickly that just mentioning a shopping trip was not enough to convince immigration officials. They had to also memorize the names of restaurants and stores as well as their hours of operation and location. Where possible, these workers even had to learn how to get to these businesses using public transportation. BCC holders like these invent detailed stories to provide convincing evidence of their innocuous visits to relatives or shopping centres in San Diego County. Diego Sánchez, a twenty-three year old internal migrant from Jalisco, for example, told me about his friends who lost their border crossing privileges because they were not prepared when questioned by immigration officials. He explained how you must pay attention to everything if you are to trick the border guards, "Another strategy is to always carry money – approximately $100 dollars – because it would be ridiculous to say you are going shopping but you have no money."

BCC holders who violate the terms of their card do everything to avoid raising any suspicion of working unlawfully in the US. Viviana Ramos, a twenty-three year old crosser, came across the border on Sundays, travelled to Los Angeles, and worked in a restaurant from Monday through Thursday. Viviana always asked a friend with US citizenship to transport her suitcase so that immigration officials would not question why she brought luggage. She recalls:

> On Sunday, I remember that we would get in line [at the international port of entry] and we were all heading to work and well yes one would get nervous because I would cross with everyone who was going to work and they are going to find out that I do not have any papers. But I had a friend who was a really good friend of mine and she was a US citizen. She used to always cross my suitcase for me because I could not cross my suitcase and I would then get in

> a different line so that they would not think that I did not have any papers.

By handing her suitcase off to a US citizen, Viviana avoided extensive questioning from immigration officials. Unless BCC holders have a special permit, they are only allowed to shop and visit relatives within a twenty-five mile radius of the US-Mexico border, so a suitcase would certainly raise alarm.

Other BCC crossers employed strategies, such as never carrying lunch bags or cheque stubs, to conceal evidence that they were working in the US. Omar Gallegos, a twenty-seven year old internal migrant, has successfully crossed the border for four years. During that time, he said he has witnessed many friends lose their BCCs while attempting to smuggle their work uniform in a purse or backpack. Watching these 'common sense mistakes' made Omar realize that he needed to conceal his US-based occupation. He said:

> Oh, about our uniforms, we had to hide them over there [in the US restaurant], because you could not cross with a uniform, and it was really difficult because you had to leave them in a place and we had to tell someone who could cross [to help us]... someone who could cross and wash the uniforms because we could not cross with the uniforms.

Like Omar, Miguel Alemán has been crossing the border for years and has developed various strategies to travel without raising suspicion. When he arrives at the port of entry, his main goal is to erase any possible signs that he has any affiliation with employers or friends in the US. As he puts it:

> Well... first, I never carry nobody's telephone numbers in the United States not even my work number, never. I never carry business cards from work. Everything can compromise you. You never want to show that you have a relationship to a restaurant or that you know people in the US. If you want to have the number of friends in the US, you should have the area code as 664 for here [in Tijuana] and not 619 [San Diego's area code], that you know are the right numbers so that they cannot trick you. Because I have friends who this happened to and they took away their BCC.

Miguel points to what I heard time and time again. Namely, the strategies that BCC holders adapted were largely the result of mistakes made by others. BCC holders carefully study these slips and alter their border crossing behaviours and fictitious stories to convince immigration officials into believing that their purposes are legitimate. The stories I have shared illustrate that border policing does not end unauthorized crossings; rather, it reinvents the mechanisms by which people cross borders for employment.

Conclusion

Before Gatekeeper, Tijuana was the preferred border crossing location for undocumented migrants on their way to work in the US. Border enforcement studies have shown that increased policing rerouted undocumented migration patterns from Tijuana to the Sonoran desert and altered the strategies that documented migrants employed to enter the US. This article focused on the experiences of people who crossed the border to work without authorization in the US. Specifically, I focused on the experiences of undocumented crossers who entered without inspection. I compared their experiences to new generations of border crossers whose only means of entry is the (mis)use of BCCs designed for casual visitors (not workers). By comparing these groups with detailed examples, I create a picture of the constantly changing strategies migrants employ to cross borders.

I found that during the open border era, one group of undocumented crossers either crossed alone or relied on smugglers to enter the US labour market. This finding is consistent with migration and border enforcement studies showing the importance of social support in lowering migration risks (Massey et al. 1987; Singer and Massey 1998; Durand, Massey and Zenteno 2001). However, I identified another group of crossers who lived in Mexico but crossed to work in farms adjacent to the US-Mexico border. For these crossers, declaring their occupational affiliation to growers provided them with a ticket to the US. These findings support Spener's (2009) assertion the border crossing is not a uniform process because each social actor (family, friends, smugglers, and employers) employs a variety of border-crossing strategies leading to distinct crossing outcomes.

In contrast to undocumented crossers, documented crossers depended less on the support of others and more on BCCs that allow them to enter the US, where they work without documents. Rather than circumvent inspection, this group of crossers adopted strategies that operated within formal rules. BCC crossers had to first establish work and residential histories in Mexico. Next, they had to develop strategies that convinced immigration officials that they were not BCC violators by masking their affiliation with US employers. These findings contribute to the growing literature on border enforcement and migration studies illustrating how increased policing alters migration patterns and modes of entry (Bean et al. 1994; Hernández-León 2008; Heyman 2009). But my findings go one step further than previous literature. I have identified unique strategies documented border crossers employ to enter the US labour market. With the exception of Heyman (2009) and Hernández-León's (2008) work, BCC holders have remained invisible in the migration and border studies literature. I build on the work of other scholars by showing how migrants like these, with a legal method of entry but an unauthorized purpose for work, negotiate their encounters with border patrol agents as told through their own experiences.

By focusing on the experiences of border crossers, I ultimately address the relationship between structure and agency. Although border enforcement (structure) transformed border crossings after 1994, migrants responded with the development of new strategies (agency) to cope with the new realities of the borderlands.

Acknowledgements

I would like to express my gratitude to the editor and two anonymous reviewers who made helpful suggestions. I also want to thank Max Pfeffer who continues to be a wonderful mentor long after I left Cornell; Jackie Hagan and Ted Mouw who challenged me to become a better sociologist and incorporated me into their research projects; Liana Richardson, Jan Hendrickson-Smith, and Heather Edelblute who provided important insights after hearing my presentation at the Carolina Population Center seminar series where it all got started. I also thank Robin Paige Kreider for pointing out the strength of my research and also for her support and encouragement throughout the revision process. Finally, I would like to thank the guest editors Alice Bloch and Milena Chimienti for their support and also for inviting me to present my work at the City University London. Any final errors are solely my responsibility.

References

ALEGRÍA, T. 2002 'Demand and supply of mexican cross-border workers', *Journal of Borderlands Studies*, vol. 17, no. 1, pp. 37–55

ANDREAS, P. 2000 *Border Games: Policing the US-Mexico Divide*, Ithaca, NY: Cornell University Press

BEAN, FRANK D., CHANOVE, ROLAND, CUSHING, ROBERT, G., DE LA GARZA, RODOLFO, FREEMAN, GARY, P., HAYNES, CHARLES, W. and SPENER, DAVID 1994 *Illegal Mexican Migration and the US/Mexico Border: The Effects of Operation Hold the Line in El Paso/Juarez*, Austin, TX: Population Research Center, University of Texas at Austin

BUSTAMANTE, J. A. 1990 'Undocumented migration from Mexico to the United States: preliminary findings of the Zapata Canyon project', in F. D. Bean, B. Edmonston and J. S. Passel (eds), *Undocumented Migration to the United States: IRCA and the Experience of the 1980s*, Santa Monica, CA: Rand Corporation

CHAVEZ, L. R. 1992 *Shadowed Lives: Undocumented Immigrants in American Society*, Fort Worth, TX: Harcourt Brace Jovanovich College Publishers

CORNELIUS, W. A. 1989 'Impacts of the 1986 US immigration law on emigration from rural Mexican sending communities', *Population and Development Review*, vol. 15, no. 4, pp. 689–705

——— 2005 'Controlling "unwanted" immigration: lessons from the United States, 1993-2004', *Journal of Ethnic and Migration Studies*, vol. 31, no. 4, pp. 775–94

DONATO, K., WAGNER, B. and PATTERSON, E. 2008 'The cat and mouse game at the Mexico-US border: gendered patterns and recent shifts', *International Migration Review*, vol. 42, no. 2, pp. 330–59

DUNN, T. 1996 *The Militarization of the US-Mexican border, 1978-1992: Low Intensity Conflict Doctrine Comes Home*, Austin, TX: Center for Mexican American Studies, University of Texas at Austin

DURAND, J., MASSEY, D. S. and ZENTENO, R. M. 2001 'Mexican immigration to the United States: continuities and changes', *Latin American Research Review*, vol. 36, no. 1, pp. 107–27

ESCHBACH, KARL, HAGAN, JACQUELINE, RODRIGUEZ, NESTOR, HERNÁNDEZ-LEON, RUBÉN and BAILEY, STANLEY 1999 'Death at the border', *International Migration Review*, vol. 33, no. 2, pp. 430–54

FUSSELL, E. 2004 'Sources of Mexico's migration stream: rural, urban, and border migrants to the United States', *Social Forces*, vol. 82, no. 3, pp. 937–67

GATHMAN, CHRISTINA 2008 'Effects of enforcement on illegal markets: evidence from migrant smuggling along the Southwestern border', *Journal of Public Economics*, vol. 92 (2008), pp. 1926–41

HERNÁNDEZ-LEÓN, R. 2008 *Metropolitan Migrants: The Migration of Urban Mexicans to the United States*, Berkeley, CA: University of California Press

HERZOG, L. A. 1995 'Border commuter workers and transfrontier metropolitan structure along the US-Mexico border', in O. J. Martinez (ed.), *US-Mexico Borderlands: Historical and Contemporary Perspectives*, Wilmington, DE: A Scholarly Resources Inc. Imprint

HEYMAN, J. M. 2001 'Class and classification at the US-Mexico border', *Human Organization*, vol. 60, no. 2, pp. 128–40

——— 2002 'US immigration officers of Mexican ancestry as Mexican Americans, citizens, and immigration police', *Current Anthropology*, vol. 43, no. 3, pp. 479–507

——— 2009 'Trust, privilege, and discretion in the governance of the US borderlands with Mexico', *Canadian Journal of Law and Society*, vol. 24, no. 3, pp. 367–90

MASSEY, DOUGLAS S., ALARCÓN, RAFAEL, DURAND, JORGE and GONZALES, HUMBERTO 1987 *Return to Aztlan: The Social Process of International Migration from Western Mexico*, Berkeley and Los Angeles, CA: University of California Press

MASSEY, D. S., DURAND, J. and MALONE, N. J. 2002 *Beyond Smoke and Mirrors: Mexican Immigration in an Era of Free Trade*, New York: Russell Sage Foundation

MINES, R. 1981 *Developing a Community Tradition of Migration to the United States: A Field Study in Rural Zacatecas, Mexico, and California Settlement Areas*, Monographs in US-Mexican Studies 3, La Jolla, CA: Program in United States-Mexican Studies

NEVINS, J. 2002 *Operation Gatekeeper: The Rise of the 'Illegal Alien' and the Making of the US-Mexico Boundary*, New York: Routledge

SINGER, A. and MASSEY, D. S. 1998 'The social process of undocumented border crossing among Mexican migrants', *International Migration Review*, vol. 32, no. 3, pp. 561–92

SPENER, D. 2009 *Clandestine Crossings: Migrants and Coyotes on the Texas-Mexico Border*, Ithaca, NY: Cornell University Press

YOUNG, E. 1994 'The impact of IRCA on settlement patterns among Mixtec migrants in Tijuana, Mexico', *Journal of Borderlands Studies*, vol. IX, no. 2, pp. 109–28

ZABIN, C. and HUGHES, S. 1995 'Economic integration and labor flows: stage migration in farm labor markets in Mexico and the United States', *International Migration Review*, vol. 39, no. 2, pp. 395–422

Mobilization of irregular migrants in Europe: a comparative analysis

Milena Chimienti

Abstract

Why and how do those who by definition seek to avoid the attention of the public and who lack resources manage to mobilize collectively? Comparing the situation of irregular migrants in three European cities (Copenhagen, London and Paris), this article aims to provide some understanding of the reasons for the mobilization, or absence of mobilization, of irregular migrants. It also seeks to explore the processes of development in these movements. In exploring the determinants and modes of irregular migrant mobilizations, this paper builds on Axel Honneth's theory of recognition and expands the analysis provided by theories of social movements of the passage from individual suffering to collective action.

Introduction

Mistrust, illegality and a lack of resources tend to make collective action by irregular migrants seemingly impossible, or at least unlikely. And yet, in many European countries, instances of collective action by these people exist.

Research on irregular migrants' social movements has, however, only provided theoretically limited accounts of the reasons for their mobilization and has focused empirically on national or local cases.[1] Through a cross-national comparative analysis of the mobilization of irregular migrants, this article aims at an understanding of why collective action by people in situations of vulnerability – who by definition seek to avoid the attention of authorities – occurs. It also seeks to offer insights as to how people with few economic, social and legal resources manage to mobilize collectively.

This article draws on qualitative research on the mobilizations of contemporary vulnerable groups, including irregular migrants in Paris, London and Copenhagen, conducted between 2008 and 2009. It is based mainly on semi-structured interviews with spokespeople from irregular migrants' organizations and (at times when there was no mobilization) with representatives of NGOs supporting irregular migrants, as well as with representatives of the immigration authorities (a total of 30 interviews).[2]

Theories on mobilization have for a long time been dichotomized into structural and individual explanations. The former have explained the development of mobilizations through the availability of opportunity structures, which have been either strictly limited to political parties (Eisinger 1973) or associated with state institutions (Ireland 1994). Derivatives of political opportunity structure theory (POS) have extended this explicative model to discursive opportunities (Koopmans et al. 2005), and how the population provides the legitimacy necessary for the mobilization to become publicly known. Later forms have focused on individual attitudes, including psycho-social approaches looking at the role of emotions in the emergence of mobilization (see, for the recent period, Goodwin, Jasper and Polletta 2001).

Despite their interest, these approaches have generated criticisms including, in the case of POS, 'political reductionism' and the inability to understand what preceded the mobilization (Melucci 1989),[3] and, in the case of psycho-social approaches, the risk of over-psychologization of human action. Although in the past two decades theories have tried to go beyond this dichotomy to better understand the dynamic leading from 'conflicts to action' (see for instance Melucci 1996), research still struggles to explain the passage from individual to collective action (Della Porta and Diani 2005 [1999], p. 13). In order to expand this understanding we will combine these theories on social movements with Honneth's Hegelian theory of recognition (2005 [1995]). The approach of this philosophy will be useful in three ways.

First, Honneth allows us to consider both the objective and subjective determinants of mobilization, going beyond the dichotomy present in former social movement theories.[4] For Honneth social justice includes different spheres (affective, socio-economic and legal) each of which requires recognition and is of equal importance. In this perspective, objective rights are as important as personal relations for social justice. This theory values the discourse of the agents and allows us to understand the objective context through their subjective perspective.

Secondly, considering both objective and subjective contexts, this approach offers a fuller understanding of the reasons for mobilization and explains the passage from individual suffering to collective action. For Honneth the trigger for action is primarily the denial of recognition, where 'individuals' broadly "moral" expectations are "violated"' (2005 [1995], p. xi). The struggle for recognition is moral because it is generated by the 'feeling of outrage' and therefore implies 'normative judgments about the legitimacy of social arrangements', which are formulated according to individuals' expectations of recognition (Honneth 2005 [1995], p. xii). These normative judgements are volatile, as are people's expectations, because they are formulated according to their objective and subjective contexts (Honneth 2005 [1995], pp. xii, 160). This moral root is also related to the intersubjective basis of recognition. For Honneth, one's idea of one's self is dependent on the confirmation of one's value by others (2005 [1995], p. 92). Conversely, a shared experience of disrespect is a precondition for action for social change.[5]

Thirdly, the theory of recognition highlights the importance of both opportunities and suffering. For Honneth, suffering (related to a lack of recognition) is an engine of social change, envisaged as an insult that removes individuals' value and therefore stimulates them to overcome this threat (2005 [1995], p. 160). But this potential depends both on the shared awareness among a minority of the insult, and on the objective context: the claim must appear legitimate enough to be heard and supported by society.

With this theoretical grounding in mind, we explore the basis of several mobilizations of irregular migrants, looking at the objective and subjective contexts in which each took place. In each city we studied this objective context through the lens of the local migratory regime, which we assumed was the origin of the suffering of irregular migrants. In other words we identified which changes in the migratory regime were followed by a mobilization.

For the subjective context that triggered these mobilizations, we examine the *claims* made by the irregular migrants involved, considering the extent to which they relate to a denial of recognition and the type of identity displayed by the protestors, looking at the role of intersubjectivity in their struggle.

In order to explore the modes and development processes of these movements we draw on theories of mobilization. Our aim is to identify the role of opportunities offered by the context, and of the independence of the irregular migrants involved in them. We look at three aspects of these mobilizations in particular: their *repertoire of action*; their *internal organization*, for instance, their decision-making process; and their *coalition building* with allies.

Migratory regime

This section will consider the objective contexts of mobilization. We will examine, in each country of focus, the changes in migratory regimes over the past few decades which provoked (or did not provoke) a mobilization.

France: from irregular migration as a legal way to migrate, to 'chosen migration' policy

Among the countries studied, France shows the most extreme shift from the tolerance of irregular migrants to conflict. For 30 years (1945–1974) France implemented an open immigration policy in order to meet its economic and demographic needs, and in response to the de-colonization process, which tolerated and even recognized illegality as a mode of migration (Weil 1995). The period between 1972 and 1980 marked an important change in this policy.

In 1972 Marcellin-Fontanet's Circular forbade the *a posteriori* regularization of irregular migrants which had been common before this period, and limited work permits to skilled migrants. This was followed in 1974 by the barring of new flows of migrant workers (Weil 1995, p. 720). In 1980 Bonnet's Circular led to large-scale forced deportation of those without the required documents. These laws marked the beginning of irregular migrants' mobilization in France, and were followed by a series of regularizations (see Siméant 1998).

This restrictive period was followed by a short period of openness regarding irregular migration, symbolized by the 'grand' regularization by Pierre Mauroy, which ended with the 'zero immigration' policy of Minister of the Interior Charles Pasqua. This policy made regularization impossible for two groups of people who had entered irregularly, who previously had been able, in theory, to achieve it: those who had entered the country without documents but had since had children in France, and those who had been living in France for more than 10 years. This law curtailed irregular migrants' job opportunities and therefore made their lives impossible, similarly to the earlier laws. One of the measures put in place in the mid-1990s was to order 'police and public transport employees to check the identity papers of any and all "suspicious" and "foreign-looking" individuals' (Iskander 2007, p. 324). The second measure, which aimed to complicate the employment of irregular immigrants, contained 'the provision that criminalized aiding and abetting' irregular immigrants, making 'nervous business owners [...] reluctant to hire' undocumented workers (Iskander 2007, p. 324).

Ensuing laws followed this logic until recently. Despite a short period of regularization, the three new laws passed between 2002 and

2007 instituted much stronger measures against irregular migration, tightening all rules of admission and the possibility of regularization. Since then the revocation of permission to stay and the obligation to leave the country have been combined into one potential ruling. The new law launched by Minister of Immigration Brice Hortefeux in 2007 authorized genetic tests of potential migrants who apply for family reunification in order to prove their kinship. It further tightened the criteria for admission and regularization, including shortening the deadline for submission of the request, and limiting access to the labour market to a list of 29 professions.

Despite these important changes in the migratory regime, active repression through workplace raids, detention and deportation is used more as a deterrent, in an isolated way, than implemented systematically (Schuster 2011), allowing some space for resistance, as we will show in the second part of this article.

United Kingdom: from liberal immigration policy to managed migration

In contrast to the French context, irregular migration is a relatively new issue in the UK, although it has become a central focus of British immigration policy since 2004. Until the last decade, the country had observed a more liberal immigration policy than other European member states, permitting people to migrate legally. The colonial past of the UK has, like that of France, framed its migration regime in terms of admission, integration and race relations policies, since, when post-war flows of Europeans proved insufficient, migrant recruitment had to be extended to black colonial workers (Solomos 2003).

This liberal British migration policy, however, has been in retreat since 1962. Since then a series of immigration acts have been promulgated in order to limit the settlement of Black and Asian people, restricting settlement visas to family reunion cases only (Solomos 2003). The 1988 Immigration Act marked a clear intention to end immigration from Commonwealth countries (Solomos 2003). This restriction limited the admission of newcomers but also bound those who managed to migrate to their employment contracts, making them more dependent on their employers, and making possible all sorts of abuse on the part of the latter (Anderson 2010). This situation led to a first mobilization of irregular migrants in London in 1984, as we will discuss later.

The 1999 Asylum and Immigration Act marked another important change. It increased the penalties for illegal entry and marked the beginning of the current fight against irregular migration. However, irregular migrants' mobilization against this policy only began in the 2000s when laws against irregular work became more severe following EU policy changes (Triandafyllidou 2010). Whereas under the Asylum and Immigration Act of 1996 employing an irregular migrant was considered a criminal offence (Flynn 2005), the 2006 Act not only increased the fine for employers of irregular migrants (to £10,000 per unauthorized worker), but also 'made it a criminal offence to take on and/or to continue to employ a person known to lack permission to work in the UK, leading to prosecution and a maximum two year prison sentence' (MRN 2008, p. 8). This law extended the responsibilities of employers so that they must now conduct repeated document checks.

Despite the curtailing since the mid-2000s of irregular migrants' rights to work, education and more recently healthcare, active repression through, for instance, systematic raids of workplaces or systematic deportation is not implemented as is the case in France (Home Office 2009). Nevertheless there have been significant impacts on those who have experienced these measures (Bloch, Sigona and Zetter 2010). The bureaucratic system in the UK allows irregular migrants some interstices of freedom. Jordan and Düvell (2002), for instance, note that there is neither compulsory registration nor any legal obligation to carry an identity card. Many documents (income tax receipts, pay slips, etc.) can serve as a proof of identity. Furthermore, the UK has limited experience with regularization programmes compared to France (Triandafyllidou 2010). This context in part explains why irregular migrants' mobilization is a recent and less extensive phenomenon than in France, as we will illustrate later.

Denmark: an 'anti-immigration regime' since 1980 and criminalization of irregular migrants

Denmark still does not consider itself an immigration country. Until 1970 the Danish population was relatively homogeneous, a characteristic which is at the root of its welfare system (Hedetoft 2006). Until recently immigration flows were regulated and came mostly through a guest worker programme from other Nordic and Western countries (Hedetoft 2006).

At the end of the guest worker programme in the 1970s the country faced an increase of asylum seekers. This rapid immigration growth and the diversity that characterized it led to 'anti-immigrant feelings' and, since the mid-1980s, to 'xenophobic politics', which found expression in a series of laws passed by the new Danish government in 2001 circumscribing immigrants' and refugees' lives (Rydgren 2004; Berggren 2007). Among the most debated was the law restricting family reunion (Berggren 2007, p. 381).[6]

Danish asylum law has also become one of the most restrictive in Europe (Clandestino Project 2009, p. 16). Since the Danish law of 2002, asylum seekers who are ineligible but cannot be returned to their country of origin for security reasons are kept in detention centres without any right to education or work and with access only to a parallel healthcare system. Denmark went further than most other European countries by including child asylum seekers in these restrictions. They are, as are their parents, excluded from the general Danish education and healthcare systems (ECRI 2006).

The situation in Denmark also tends toward the extreme criminalization of irregular migrants, according to the NGO representatives interviewed. First, the control of irregular migrants and the deportation of those who have been arrested seem to be more effective than in France and the UK, where these are not priorities for the police and are applied more as a symbolic deterrence measure, through isolated checks on specific economic sectors. Similarly, in France and the UK irregular migrants who are caught are not systematically deported, which seems to be the practice in Denmark (one that has been denounced by, among others, Amnesty International, in 2008).

In other words Denmark appears to have one of the most restrictive migratory regimes in north-west Europe regarding both regular and irregular migration, which has faced only recent and minimal criticism (Berggren 2007, pp. 384–6).

***

This brief overview of the main changes in the French, English and Danish migratory regimes highlights three interesting phenomena. First, as noted by Laubenthal (2007), restrictiveness toward irregular migrants is not enough to explain their mobilization: there must be a shift from (relative) tolerance to restrictiveness so that the new situation appears unfair enough both to the victims of this policy and to the rest of the population to justify a mobilization. Whereas these three countries have developed similarly restrictive immigration policies, France and the UK's contrasting past migration regimes offer more interstices for the tolerance and legitimacy of such mobilizations than that of Denmark. Secondly, using this logic, conflicts and suffering are more relevant than opportunities in explaining the emergence of mobilization. Thirdly, mobilization appears to be triggered more by economic imperatives than by political ones: when irregular migrants are barred from labour markets they start to mobilize. We will illustrate these points further in the next section.

Mobilization: genesis, focus of claims, internal and external organization

This section will explore the subjective context of mobilizations and how they enter the public sphere.

Paris: normalization of the mobilization process

In Paris many irregular migrant mobilizations have taken place since the 1970s. As a consequence the French government set up a regularization process, creating several amnesties (Siméant 1998; Laubenthal 2007). Since this period, however, these social movements have not decreased as the amnesties did not reach all irregular migrants, and because new migrants arrived or existing migrants became irregular after they lost their permit of stay, this resulted in new mobilizations. We studied two current cases: the *Forgotten of Saint-Paul* and the *Neuvième Collectif.*[7] However to understand the genesis of these movements we need to look at their recent (1990s) predecessors.

Genesis of mobilization and focus of claims. These earlier mobilizations occurred just after the implementation of the 1993 Pasqua laws which curtailed job opportunities, and were primarily motivated by exclusion from the labour market. This can be illustrated by the movement of the Chinese and Turkish from the Sentier, which started when garment industry jobs suddenly became 'off limits to anyone without legal work permits' (Iskander 2007, p. 310). Moreover, the Parisian irregular migrants' movement did not call for the state to improve informal labour markets, but for re-entry to the legitimate labour market (Iskander 2007, pp. 318, 330), and thus for a right to live and survive despite their irregularity.

The focus on labour access is still central to the current mobilization in Paris:

> We just demand the right to work [. . .] I am here for 20 years, I've always worked, paid my taxes and that's it. (Interview with a member of the *Neuvième Collectif*, 4 September 2009, Paris)

In other words, irregular migrants start to mobilize when they have nothing to lose. They perceive their situation as unjust when they lose the right to work, which is only then experienced as a denial of their economic and historical links with the country. Most irregular migrants' movements cease to exist when some of the members are regularized, which supports the idea that they primarily concern access to the labour market.

However the shift to collective action occurs only when irregular migrants become aware of a common experience of injustice.

> When I lost my job I began to talk to others [*sans-papiers*] and I understood that this country has a problem [. . .] I remember that it was a relief not to feel alone anymore [. . .] (Interview with a member of the *Neuvième Collectif*, 4 September 2009, Paris)

This shared awareness occurs, as illustrated by this interviewee, through discussions with others in the same situation that define the cause of individual suffering, rationalize it and turn into anger, which is only then translated into collective action with the hope of change.

Identity. Irregular migrants' mobilizations in Paris are often based on a minimal common denominator, i.e. irregularity, rather than ethnicity or nationality. The *Neuvième Collectif*, for example, is composed of people who came to France in search of work, rejected asylum seekers, students whose permit of stay expired at the end of their studies, and families with French-born children who have been in France for many years, all of different nationalities and working in different economic sectors. This plurality is chosen by the movement, which perceives it as a strength, believing it increases their visibility and the legitimacy of their claim. The conflation of the control of irregular migration with asylum by the migratory regime since 1989 helps to bring the two groups together.

Repertoire of actions. The repertoire of actions of irregular migrants in France has been quite similar over time: for example in the 1970s, 'they made a public demand for residence and work permits and when their appeals were formally denied, they occupied a public space, usually a church, and began a hunger strike' (Iskander 2007, p. 315). They have legitimated their claims by reminding the public of their historical link with France and their contribution to the national economy:

> We are first workers before to be irregular migrants, we are not criminal, we are useful for the economy of this country. (Interview with a member of the *Neuvième Collectif*, 4 September 2009, Paris)

The human rights discourse (i.e. rights claims justified by the fact of being human) and extreme actions are used only as a last recourse. These extreme actions highlight both the despair and suffering of these groups, and the lack of other ways to make their voices heard publicly, as shown by this statement:

> We know this decision [to go on a hunger strike] is grave, but because we are desperate, hundreds of us are willing to resort to this ultimate step. (Opening line of the *Troisième Collectif*'s mimeographed leaflets, quoted in Iskander 2007, p. 328)

Although only a minority of the protestors have gone on hunger strike, the resort to such extreme measures also underlines how unfair they perceive their situation to be, and conversely how legitimate they judge their claim to be.

Organization. Another characteristic of these Parisian mobilizations was that initially many were self-organized, and several remained so throughout. The current mobilizations of the *Forgotten of Saint-Paul* and the *Neuvième Collectif* were both launched by former protestors from mobilizations disbanded after the regularization of a significant proportion of their participants: the *Forgotten of Saint-Paul* was created in 2008 by 58 former participants of the *Collectif des Sans-Papiers du Département des Hauts-de-Seine*, also known as CSP 92 (itself created after the disbanding of a former mobilization in 1996); and the *Neuvième Collectif* was created in 1997 by 5–10 members of the former collective of the St Bernard Church (1996), who, unlike the majority of members of the former collective, had not been regularized.

Representatives of both the organizations studied argue that self-organization has often been motivated by migrants' lack of trust in other supporters. They fear being instrumentalized and feel betrayed, as was the case with half the members of the St Bernard Church, who have been only partially supported by left-wing parties and trade unions. Self-organization has also given the group more freedom to direct their claims to all political parties, which according to the following interviewee have the same problematic vision of migration:

> Our claims are carried out by the concerned persons themselves [. . .] as we do not have any labels [. . .] we can question both right and left wing political parties [. . .] both type of parties associate migration to insecurity, both are demagogic. (Interview with one of the spokespeople of the *Neuvième Collectif*, 29 November 2008, Paris)

The *Neuvième Collectif* is also independent logistically: they meet in a space that is not attached to a church or association, and are financed mainly by members' contributions. This relative independence calls for responsibility: members are all considered to be in charge of their own situation and claims. This also means that they will not accept (in theory at least) case-by-case or small-group regularizations, but instead appeal for regularization collectively.

In the case of the *Forgotten of Saint-Paul*, self-organization is less chosen than imposed. The relative failure of the CSP 92 discouraged their supporters and provoked their withdrawal during the re-formation of the movement. This can also be explained by the saturation of irregular migrants' allies in France, as argued by Siméant (1998), since their mobilization can be dated from the 1970s.

Whether self-organization is chosen or imposed, these movements, needing allies both for logistical support and to legitimize their claims, try to motivate potential supporters to join them. Parisian irregular migrants have benefited since the beginning of their mobilization from the support of intellectuals and artists (see Mathieu 2009), and several trade unions have lent support in exchange for the movement's support of their claim for better working conditions.[8] If the *Neuvième Collectif* continues to be self-organized, it will do so with larger support networks. One of the group's spokespeople explains the movement of '*sans*' (literally 'without') they are trying to mobilize:

> We tried to find [common grounds] with other social movements: the unemployed, the homeless and in general the movements of the precarious. The sans-papiers are the precarious among the precarious, they are therefore the first reached by the general precariousness (précarisation). It is important to create solidarity networks with other social movements [in order to invert this trend]. (Interview with one of the spokespeople of the *Neuvième Collectif*, 29 November 2008, Paris)

Another characteristic of these mobilizations is that they are numerous but ephemeral. As soon as some of the members become regularized, the movement disappears completely or is reborn as another coalition. This characteristic is not particular to Parisian mobilizations, but becomes more obvious in this context because of their plurality: each recent protest seems to have occurred just after the disabling of the previous one. This is the case with the *Troisième Collectif*, and with the two current mobilizations studied.

This snapshot shows that these mobilizations have become a 'normal' process in France, as explained by an NGO representative:

> People know that here the law is never applied mathematically, it is never just yes or no. Migrants know that between these two, the administration always has some space for interpretation. . . . They all know that there have been regularizations, and that there is a chance to obtain one. (Interview, Groupe d'information et de soutien des immigrés (GISTI), 2 June 2003, quoted in Laubenthal 2007, p. 109)

The lack of a global solution, with a timely response involving regularizations, is perceived as unfair by irregular migrants. This context is therefore likely to continue to generate protests.

London: isolated mobilizations of irregular migrants and mediation by NGOs

London has seen few mobilizations by irregular migrants or regularizations in recent decades.

Genesis and focus of claims. One of the first such mobilizations in London occurred in 1984. It was launched by the Commission for Filipino Migrant Workers (CFMW) in West London which, noticing common problems among these workers, set up a group in 1984 under the name of Waling Waling, which then became self-organized (Anderson 2010, p. 60). This mobilization led in 1997 to the regularization of some of the irregular workers. In contrast to the French case, however, these regularizations were not collective but on a case-by-case basis (Anderson 2010).

Current mobilizations show a similar trend. The interviews we conducted with representatives of the Chinese Immigration Concerned Committee (CICC), Ukrainian Support Network, Cameroun Support Network, and NGOs advocating for irregular migrants' rights (including the Migrants' Rights Network) show that individual migrants' claims are often taken up by NGOs or community organizations involving employers. The primary role of these organizations is to share information, but irregular migrants have recently become a main focus for them due to their increased repression. Thus public protest and mobilization represent only a secondary activity.

The recent mobilizations of irregular migrants occurred after police raids on economic sectors known to employ them. This indicates, as in the Parisian case, that irregular migrants' claims are triggered when they are barred from working and threatened with deportation. For instance in October 2007, several police raids occurred in Chinese restaurants in London's Chinatown. The employers of Chinese irregular migrants reacted to this raid by creating an organization (the CICC) to fight the points system that does not allow them to employ the low-skilled workers they need.

More recently, in June 2009, irregular migrant cleaners were subjected to a workplace raid and arrested, which led to another mobilization. This was orchestrated by a campaign that aimed to organize low-paid workers (especially cleaners) in the City of London, led by unions and community networks.[9] These campaigns sought to secure better pay and conditions for workers, and involved all categories of workers, including irregular migrants. More generally, NGOs such as the Migrants' Rights Network (MRN) organized protests, petitions and public events to advocate for irregular migrants' rights.[10]

In other words irregular migrants' mobilizations in London, in contrast to those in Paris, have been organized in collaboration with NGOs or ethnic minority communities whose members mainly have legal permission to stay.

Identity. Another contrast with the Parisian case concerns the ethnic or national roots of the mobilization. The support of long-term ethnic communities in the UK helps to explain why past and current mobilizations are at first more likely to be ethnically or nationally organized than in France. However these organizations are open to migrants of different countries of origin, or at least situate their claims beyond the specific ethnic or national groups concerned, recognizing the rights of all irregular migrants. For instance, although CICC represents a majority of Chinese employers of irregular migrants and a minority of Chinese irregular migrants, their claim encompasses the whole catering sector.

Organization and repertoire of actions. The fact that the London mobilization was developed in close collaboration with allies can be explained by community groups' strong support in the UK,[11] but also ironically by the support of irregular migrants' employers. The recent increase of repression toward employers of irregular migrants has pushed them to mobilize alongside their irregular employees. One of our interviewees from CICC commented: 'this is the first time that employers' and employees' interests coincide'. Moreover, the absence of mobilization by irregular migrants themselves can be explained by their ability to access the labour market, even irregularly, and the relative tolerance they have experienced in the UK. They manage to cope in these conditions, since as long as they remain discreet they are not ordinarily hunted down. Finally, the rarity of collective regularization so far in the UK might incentivize migrants to stay invisible rather than to mobilize. This economic access and the moderate repression used until recently might also explain why UK mobilizations have a less extreme repertoire of action.

The embeddedness of irregular migrants' claims in the larger migrant community (who have legal status) or NGOs may also explain why mobilizations for their rights are more likely to last. Although those who manage to become regularized generally leave the organization, the community, and especially the NGO, may nevertheless continue to fight for their rights.

Copenhagen: invisibility of irregular migrants and absence of mobilization

The situation in Copenhagen offers a counter-example to help us understand why a mobilization of irregular migrants might take place, since none has so far occurred there. This is somewhat paradoxical since the country has one of the most restrictive policies in Europe (Clandestino Project 2009). Reasons for this lack of collective action can be found in both the objective and subjective contexts.

Whereas all three countries studied here have developed restrictive immigration policies, newcomers in Denmark did not benefit from the struggle for rights that occurred in the UK and France with the inflow of migrants from former colonies during the *Trente Glorieuses*, and equally through these countries' feeling of responsibility toward them. This past generated a degree of sensitivity regarding migrants in France and the UK, supported by long-settled ethnic minorities, although it also generated racist movements (Weil 1995 [1991]; Solomos 2003). This context created a 'cultural resonance' (Benford and Snow 2000, p. 619) that made irregular migrants' claims appear more legitimate to the public in France and the UK, in contrast to Denmark. As highlighted by the following statement, even migrants' advocacy and support organizations 'do not know how to' help irregular migrants.

> We don't know how to support these people [irregular migrants] [. . .] We would like to advocate for their lack of rights, but we are afraid that the consequences could be to send them home [. . .]. (Interview with a representative of an NGO, 30 March 2009, Copenhagen)

NGOs focus on rejected asylum seekers who are threatened with deportation while still at risk in their country of origin. Other irregular migrants whose motivations are more economic than political are not seen as a legitimate cause, as a representative of an activist association mentioned:

> It is not illegal to help people, but it is illegal to assist them to become underground, for instance to rent a flat. We never encourage people to get underground, i.e. irregular. It is not a solution to get irregular. It is a hopeless situation. (Interview with a representative of the Committee for Underground Refugees, 30 March 2009, Copenhagen)

As a consequence, Danish activists, intellectuals and artists have not yet engaged in the cause, in contrast to the French and English cases.

Moreover the current Danish immigration policy does not offer any access point for collective action: deportations of irregular migrants are implemented more systematically, so that rejected asylum seekers who cannot be returned to their country of origin for safety reasons, but are no longer regular, are therefore kept in detention centres (since the 2002 law; see ECRI 2006). According to several interviewees, if irregular migrants launched a protest, their papers would be checked and they would be automatically arrested and deported.

The lack of opportunities in the objective context, i.e. the lack of social support and legitimation, is not the only reason for the absence of mobilization. The heterogeneity of irregular migrant groups has not so far allowed them to develop a shared awareness of their common suffering. Whereas in Paris and London irregular migrants protest together regardless of their former legal situation, ethnicity or nationality, this common identity is lacking in Copenhagen. Rejected asylum seekers benefit from NGO support and thus enjoy more legitimacy, which tends to discourage them from forming a coalition with other irregular migrants. The extreme precariousness of the others' irregular status obliges them to hide and count only on themselves. There is thus no shared awareness to create a group identity and in turn make it possible to formalize collective anger. In Copenhagen, the voice of irregular migrants has therefore not (yet) reached the public sphere, even through the mediation of NGOs.

Conclusion

This article has identified some of the reasons and modes of irregular migrants' mobilization. Along with Honneth's theory of recognition (2005 [1995]), their mobilization can be explained by the objective and subjective contexts in which it takes place. This theoretical grounding allows us to understand why, despite a similarly repressive context, irregular migrants did not mobilize in all these cities to fight the immigration regime. The objective context triggers mobilization, causing the suffering that leads to moral indignation and then resistance. In our study the change from relative tolerance to repression sparks collective action, specifically when irregular migrants are barred from the labour market, which confirms Iskander's (2007) and Milkman's (2006) findings.

Pain, however, is not enough to explain resistance. In order to turn this suffering into moral indignation and therefore into collective and public action, the context has to be perceived as sufficiently unfair by the victims themselves, but also by public opinion. This involves, on the one hand, an inter-subjective dimension, and on the other, opportunities.

At the inter-subjective level irregular migrants in Paris and London became aware that they were enduring a common situation that they perceived as unfair. This shared awareness was based on a minimal common identity: the fact of being an irregular migrant and claiming the right to live in a chosen society, even irregularly. This common identity, which allows solidarity on the basis of collective action, is fragile. As we have seen in the Parisian case, the protestors are likely to leave the movement once they are regularized or, as in the case of London, the struggle might rapidly become mediated by NGOs. Such mediation, and irregular migrants' access to (irregular) labour, among other factors, render them less visible and their voice less audible.

Opportunities also play an important role in the success of the mobilization, as POS has abundantly demonstrated (Koopmans et al. 2005). The claim must appear reasonable to spark shared awareness and to be heard publicly. The shift from tolerance to repression, the historical linkages between irregular migrants' countries of origin and the countries in which their protests take place, and the responsibility or guilt this might involve, as well as their economic value, are conditions that give the claim the legitimacy to develop further. This article illustrates, however, that structural opportunities become relevant once irregular migrants share an awareness of common suffering and when their mobilization moves their claim into the public sphere.

The Copenhagen case does not meet these two main conditions, which explains the current absence of mobilization there. In Copenhagen, irregular migrants' claims are still made individually, and so have not reached the public sphere and are not supported by NGOs, whereas in Paris, mobilizations range from collective anger to NGO advocacy, and in London mobilizations seem to be carried out mainly by NGOs and ethnic community groups.

Finally, our results seem to move away from Honneth's theory in two aspects. First, solidarity among protestors appears to be instrumental, temporary and often problematic, whereas in Honneth's perspective of struggles for recognition, asymmetric relationships are neglected.[12] Secondly, although through their very existence irregular migrants are a challenge to the nationalistic sense of belonging and have the potential to question the notion of citizenship, as argued by, among others, McNevin (2009), in our cases studied, mobilization leads at best to some regularization, but is characterized by 'existential' and 'individualistic' changes rather than by structural changes in policy, as we demonstrate elsewhere (Chimienti and Solomos 2011). In other words, these mobilizations have not achieved the 'moral progress' and 'general reconciliation' encompassed in Honneth's logic of the struggle for recognition (Deranty 2003, pp. 190, 197). These caveats call for long-term empirical research on irregular migrants' mobilization, as well as further theoretical accounts to investigate to what extent such potential could be achieved, and its meaning.

Acknowledgements

Thanks to Sandro Cattacin and Mélanie Pétrémont for their participation in the research project this paper draws on. Thanks to the three anonymous reviewers, Lilian Mathieu and John Solomos for their useful comments, as well as to Linnet Taylor for proofreading this paper.

Notes

1. For a critical analysis of the literature on migrants' mobilization see Però and Solomos (2010).
2. This study was financed by the French Ministry of Public Works (Ministère de l'écologie, du développement et de l'aménagement durables).

3. It focuses on the 'how' question and does not answer the 'why' (Giugni 1995, p. 81).
4. As shown already by Marta Roca I Escoda (2010).
5. 'Hurt feelings [...] can, however, become the motivational basis for collective resistance only if subjects are able to articulate them within an intersubjective framework of interpretation that they can show to be typical for an *entire group*' (Honneth 2005 [1995], p. 163, emphasis added).
6. According to this law a spouse can join his or her partner only if they are over 24 years old, own their home or have a three-year lease on an apartment or house; if the partner in Denmark did not receive social security during the last year; if he or she has at least the equivalent of 5,300 euros in the bank and can demonstrate his or her ability to support his or her partner; and finally if they can both prove they have a greater connection to Denmark than to another country.
7. We have chosen these two mobilizations because of their different duration: the *Forgotten of Saint-Paul* began in 2008 whereas the *Neuvième Collectif* was created 13 years ago. *Saint-Paul* is the name of the church where the mobilized irregular migrants have settled; they term themselves 'Forgotten' because they were not regularized after their first mobilization (*Collectif des Sans-Papiers du Département des Hauts-de-Seine*). The name *Neuvième Collectif* (ninth collective) marks their place in the lineage of Parisian immigrant collectives, as does the name *Troisième Collectif* (third collective).
8. For instance see Dubuc (2008).
9. See www.strangersintocitizens.org.uk
10. See www.migrantsrights.org.uk
11. Ethnic minority communities whose members mainly have legal permission to stay.
12. Along with Deranty's critical perspective on Honneth (Deranty 2003, p. 191).

References

AMNESTY INTERNATIONAL 2008 'Denmark: Open letter to Danish Minister of Justice re: Denmark and diplomatic assurances against grave violations of human rights', available at: http://www.amnesty.org/en/library/info/EUR18/004/2008/en

ANDERSON, B. 2010 'Mobilizing migrants, making citizens: migrant domestic workers as political agents', *Ethnic and Racial Studies*, vol. 33, no. 1, pp. 60–74

BENFORD, R.D. and SNOW, D.A. 2000 'Framing processes and social movements: an overview and assessment', *Annual Review of Sociology*, vol. 26, pp. 611–39

BLOCH, A., SIGONA, N. and ZETTER, R. 2010 '"No right to dream": the social and economic lives of young undocumented migrants in Britain', Paul Hamlyn Foundation, available at: http://www.phf.org.uk

BERGGREN, E. 2007 'Danish xenophobia – power logic in motion', in E. Berggren, et al. (eds), *Irregular Migration, Informal Labour and Community: A Challenge for Europe*, Maastricht: Shaker, pp. 372–90

CHIMIENTI, M. and SOLOMOS, J. 2011 (forthcoming) 'Social movements of irregular migrants: the struggle for existential rights', *Globalizations*, vol. 8, no. 1

CLANDESTINO PROJECT 2009 Final Report, available at: http://clandestino.eliamep.gr/

DELLA PORTA, D. and DIANI, M. 2005 [1999] *Social Movements: An Introduction*, Oxford: Blackwell

DERANTY, J.-P. 2003 'Mésentente et reconnaissance: Honneth face à Rancière', in E. Renault and Y. Sintomer (eds), *Où en est la théorie critique?*, Paris: La Découverte, pp. 185–99

DUBUC, B. 2008 'Une instrumentalisation des sans-papiers', *L'Express*, 6 May

EISINGER, P. 1973 'The conditions of protest behavior in American cities', *American Political Science Review*, vol. 67, no. 1, pp. 11–28

EUROPEAN COMMISSION AGAINST RACISM AND INTOLERANCE (ECRI) 2006 Third Report on Denmark, available at: http://www.unhcr.org/refworld/docid/46efa2db1a.html

FLYNN, D. 2005'An historical note on labour migration policy in the UK', in Labour Migration and Employment Rights, London: Institute of Employment Rights, pp. 1–7

GIUGNI, M. 1995 *Entre stratégie et opportunités. Les nouveaux mouvements sociaux en Suisse*, Zurich: Seismo

GOODWIN, J., JASPER, J.M. and POLLETTA, F. 2001 *Passionate Politics: Emotions and Social Movements*, Chicago: University of Chicago Press

HEDETOFT, U. 2006 'More than kin and less than kind. The Danish politics of ethnic consensus and the pluricultural challenge', in J. Campbell, et al. (eds), *National Identity and the Varieties of Capitalism: The Danish Experience*, Montreal: McGill-Queens University Press, pp. 398–430

HOME OFFICE 2009 Home Office Statistical Bulletin: Control of Immigration Statistics 2008

HONNETH, A. 2005 [1995] *The Struggle for Recognition: The Moral Grammar of Social Conflicts*, Cambridge: Polity Press [first published in German in 1992]

IRELAND, P. 1994 *The Policy Challenge of Ethnic Diversity: Immigrant Politics in France and Switzerland*, Cambridge, MA: Harvard University Press

ISKANDER, N. 2007 'Informal work and protest: undocumented immigrant activism in France, 1996–2000', *British Journal of Industrial Relations*, vol. 45, no. 2, pp. 309–34

JORDAN, B. and DÜVELL, F. 2002 *Irregular Migration: The Dilemmas of Transnational Mobility*, Cheltenham: Edward Elgar

KOOPMANS, R., STATHAM, P., GIUGNI, M. and PASSY, F. 2005 *Contested Citizenship: Immigration and Cultural Diversity in Europe*, Minneapolis: University of Minnesota Press

LAUBENTHAL, B. 2007 'The emergence of pro-regularization movements in Western Europe', *International Migration*, vol. 45, no. 3, pp. 101–33

MATHIEU, L. 2009 'Le Mouvement Contre la Double Peine', in: Ch. Traïni (ed.), *Emotions… Mobilization!*, Paris: Sciences Po. Presses, pp. 37–55

MCNEVIN, A. 2009 'Contesting citizenship: irregular migrants and strategic possibilities for political belonging', *New Political Science*, vol. 31, no. 2, pp. 163–81

MELUCCI, A. 1989 *Nomads of the Present*, Philadelphia, PA: Temple University Press

—— 1996 *Challenging Codes*, Cambridge: Cambridge University Press

MIGRANTS' RIGHTS NETWORK (MRN) 2008 '"Papers please": the impact of the civil penalty regime on the employment rights of migrants in the UK', available at: http://www.migrantsrights.org.uk/

MILKMAN, R. 2006 *L.A. Story: Immigrant Workers and the Future of the U.S. Labor Movement*, New York: Russell Sage Foundation

PERÒ, D. and SOLOMOS, J. 2010 'Migrant politics and mobilization: exclusion, engagements, incorporation', *Ethnic and Racial Studies*, vol. 33, no. 1, pp. 1–18

ROCA I ESCODA, M. 2010 *La reconnaissance en chemin. L'institutionnalisation des couples homosexuels à Genève*, Zurich: Seismo

RYDGREN, J. 2002 'Explaining the emergence of radical right-wing populist parties: the case of Denmark', *West European Politics*, vol. 27, no. 3, pp. 474–502

SCHUSTER, L. 2011 '(forthcoming) 'Turning refugees into "illegal migrants": Afghan asylum seekers in Europe', *Ethnic and Racial Studies*

SIMÉANT, J. 1998 *La cause des sans-papiers*, Paris: Presses de Sciences Po

SOLOMOS, J. 2003 *Race and Racism in Britain*, 3rd edn, Basingstoke: Palgrave

TRIANDAFYLLIDOU, A. (ed.) 2010 *Irregular Migration in Europe: Myths and Realities*, Farnham: Ashgate

WEIL, P. 1995 [1991] *La France et ses étrangers, l'aventure d'une politique de l'immigration de 1938 à nos jours*, Paris: Gallimard-Folio

The negotiation of irregular migrants' right to education in Germany: a challenge to the nation-state

Barbara Laubenthal

Abstract

Despite Western European nation-states' attempts to control access to their territories, a large number of migrants live in the European immigration countries without a legal residence status. Their access to social rights is restricted by national migration control policies. Focusing on the case of Germany, this article addresses the question of which factors may, against the background of a highly restrictive migration control regime that makes explicit provisions to deny social rights to irregular migrants, encourage policy changes in the field of irregular migrants' social rights. Analysing several recent cases of successful implementation of educational rights for children without a legal residence status, the article argues that the institutional structure of a nation-state can have an important impact regarding policy changes on irregular migration. The article analyses how the interplay of the specific federal structure of the German state and the existence of the international human rights regime have served as preconditions for an improved access of irregular migrants to the right to education.

One of the issues at the core of the phenomenon of irregular migration[1] is the tension between migration control policies aiming at the prevention of irregular migration and social rights claims of irregular migrants residing in a state despite the efforts of this state to prevent their presence. Notwithstanding Western European nation-states' attempts to control access to their territory and the intensification of migration control policies during recent years (Vogel and Cyrus

2008), both economic pull factors in host countries and existing migration networks between sending and receiving countries contribute to the presence of a large number of irregular migrants in Western European countries (Sciortino 2004; Bommes 2006). However, because of their lack of a legal residence status, irregular migrants have only limited access to social, political and economic rights. 'By breaking the law *by their mere presence* irregular migrants are nearly always excluded from political, social and economic rights' (Bogusz *et al.* 2004, p. xiv, emphasis in original). Albeit to varying degrees according to the national political context, irregular migrants overwhelmingly work in informal arrangements in the low-skilled sectors of the labour market and often face a high risk of economic exploitation. Regarding their access to social rights, national legal provisions differ. In Belgium, Italy and the Netherlands, children without a legal residence status have an explicit right to education, while in Germany, France, Spain and Great Britain, their rights are only implicitly included in the legislation (PICUM 2008; Vogel and Assler 2010). In the field of health care, approaches range from almost unrestricted access to health care in Spain to highly restrictive provisions in Germany, Austria, Denmark and Sweden (Médecins du Monde 2009). However, even when social rights are formally granted, irregular migrants are often reluctant to exercise these rights for fear of being discovered and deported (Bielefeld 2006, p. 85).

Irregular migrants' lack of, or inadequate access to social rights, is a structural feature of nation-states' sovereign right involving policies to control access to their territories and sanction attempts to violate existing legal norms regarding the entry and stay of non-nationals. However, democratic nation-states' commitment to guaranteeing basic rights and the international human rights regime create and support claims for granting irregular migrants adequate access to decent working conditions, health care and education:

> One of the key dilemmas for policy-making in the realm of irregular migration is that...these two principles are difficult to reconcile....The challenge for states is to limit access to their territories without undermining the right to seek and enjoy protection. (Koser 2005, p. 4)

Both at the national and the European level, non-governmental and international organizations raise demands for improved access to social rights for irregular migrants in European immigration countries. They overwhelmingly base their demands on the existence of international human rights norms and law, postulating the universal applicability of human rights regardless of the migrants' legal status (Cholewinski 2006; Geddie and LeVoy 2009). They argue that 'the exclusion from social rights and from international human rights standards is more than problematic ... human rights are universal and undividable' (Düvell 2006, p. 17).

Consequently, research has tried to highlight the relevance of a large body of international human rights treaties[2] for national social rights policies. Studies have offered interpretations of human rights treaties such as the International Covenant on Economic, Social and Cultural Rights (1966) aiming to show an existing legal duty of nation-states to grant social rights to irregular migrants (Bogusz *et al.* 2004; Bielefeld 2006; Cholewinski 2006; Cremer 2009). They have also stressed the existence of human rights instruments that explicitly aim at improving irregular migrants' access to social rights, such as the International Convention on the Protection of the Rights of All Migrant Workers and their Families (1990). The convention underlines irregular migrants' rights to health and to education. However, its explicit aim to grant rights to irregular migrants is considered to be one of the central obstacles to its ratification (Cholewinski 1997). The convention 'suffers ... from a lack of interest: few states have ratified it and no one major immigration country has done so' (Pecoud and de Guchteneire 2004).

Regarding the right to education, the Convention on the Rights of the Child (CRC) (1990) is often evoked in order to legitimate the right of children without a legal residence status to attend school. However, it has faced problems similar to those faced by the Convention on the Protection of All Migrant Workers and their Families, as 'state parties have accompanied their ratification...with reservation or interpretative declarations intended to limit the scope of their obligations' (Schabas 1996, pp. 472–3). In 2010, more than forty countries have not fully ratified the convention.[3] Germany is among the countries that until the year 2010 had ratified the CRC only with a reservation regarding minors who do not have a right of legal residence in Germany.

Overall, as Hansen (2002) has pointed out, the material effects of international human rights legislation on improving irregular migrants' access to social rights in the European countries have remained limited: 'lacking incorporation guarantees and enforcement mechanisms, they remain non-binding public international law, often little more than a statement of normative intent'(2002, p. 264). As such, despite ratification of a large body of international human rights treaties, national migration control policies have proven to be rather resistant to policy changes in the field of social rights, and 'in most cases NGOs have not had a demonstrable impact on policy' (Koser 2005, p. 21).

However, one aspect of the relationship between human rights legislation and the granting of social rights to irregular migrants in nation-states has remained comparatively under-researched, namely the potential indirect effects of international human rights law. As Wexler (2007) has pointed out, international human rights legislation may have effects that are non-material but nonetheless important for improving irregular migrants' access to social rights:

> Human rights treaties can provide a discursive framework to help to improve the actual condition of migrants by tempering urges to otherize, dehumanize, blame migrants.... The symbolism and rhetorical power of international law itself can be quite meaningful in constructing migrants' identity through a human rights lens and contesting dominant perspectives of migrants as purely criminal or security threats. (Wexler 2007, p. 2)

These considerations on the discursive potential of international human rights law are the starting point for this paper's analysis of recent policy changes in the field of irregular migrants' social rights in Germany. The country has one of the most restrictive migration control regimes in Europe and strongly restricts irregular migrants' access to social rights (Düvell 2006; Vogel and Cyrus 2008), yet between the years 2004 and 2009 significant policy changes in the field of educational rights of irregular migrants took place in Germany. School attendance of children without a legal residence status became a topic of growing importance in public and political discourse, and regulations aiming to enable irregular children to attend school were implemented in several German federal states. These changes on the regional level took place against the background of the highly restrictive national migration control regime that explicitly contains specific provisions to exclude irregular migrants from educational and other social rights. The existence of the international human rights regime has played a significant role in bringing about these policy changes.

Focusing on several recent cases of successful implementation of educational rights for children without a legal residence status, this paper investigates how the specific federal structure of the German state and the existence of the international human rights regime have served as preconditions for improved access to the right to education for irregular migrants. It argues that, against the background of a political context that is generally characterized by several important factors counteracting the granting of social rights to irregular migrants, the existence of the international human rights regime and the institutional structure of the German state have encouraged policy changes that challenge the aims of national migration control policy.

In order to develop this argument, the first part of the article outlines the characteristics of the German migration control regime and irregular migrants' access to social rights. It then shows how, in the public sphere, human rights have served as a central frame for legitimating demands for improved access of irregular migrants to social rights. The second part discusses the relationship between the institutional structure of the German state and its migration policies, and shows by which instruments and discourses new regulations on educational rights of children were implemented. This analysis is based on a document analysis of federal states' laws, administrative regulations that were introduced between 2004 and 2009 and press statements by politicians that were published in quality newspapers and internet publications between 2004 and 2009. Furthermore, the article draws on expert interviews with the Ministry of Education of the Federal State of North Rhine-Westphalia (department of school personnel, service law and school law), and the Ministry of Education of the Federal State of Hesse (department of school law). Finally, the paper examines the factors that have encouraged the policy changes in the field of educational rights of irregular migrants, showing that, in the process of granting social rights to irregular migrants, the German national migration control regime has been challenged both by the sub-national and the international level.

Characteristics of the German migration control regime and its impact on irregular migrants' social rights

It is estimated that between 400,000 and 600,000 migrants live in Germany without a legal residence status (Vogel 2009a), while the number of children among them ranges from 8000 to 30,000 (Vogel 2009b). Irregular migrants originate from countries as diverse as Turkey, Russia, Ukraine, Serbia and Montenegro, China, India and South America (Cyrus 2008).

Germany's handling of irregular migration is among the most restrictive in Europe. For an immigration not to have a required visa or a residence title is a criminal offence, and irregular migrants face a sophisticated control system (Glorius 2006). Public institutions are able to access each other's data, and a central register of non-nationals exists that facilitates the checking of a migrant's residence status. Official registration is mandatory for all residents (Schönwälder, Sciortino and Vogel 2006, p. 39). Other European countries allow a certain degree of inclusion of irregular migrants in the welfare state, for example, Spain allows irregular migrants the right to register in a local community and to have access to health care (Médecins du Monde 2009), while in Switzerland they have the option of paying social security contributions (Laubenthal 2007a). However, in Germany no such partial tolerance structures exist. Individual or collective ways of transforming an irregular into a legal status do not exist. Although they are demanded by some civil society actors, these claims are not discussed as an option in the public sphere (Bielefeld 2006, p. 82; Bommes 2006, p. 108). Furthermore, since 2005, the federal government's activities in the field of integration have been accompanied by intense coverage of the topic in the German media, with media discourses on irregular migration overwhelmingly focusing on European migration control policies, dominated by subjects such as human smuggling and organized crime (Bielefeld 2006, p. 108; Laubenthal and Nieland 2007; PICUM 2009).

At the same time, the activities of civil society organizations in the field of migration control policies are characterized by a low degree of politicization of irregular migration. Political campaigns of NGOs either focus on German asylum policies and the situation of rejected asylum-seekers with a precarious residence status ('*Geduldete*') or they concentrate on the situation of irregular migrants at the EU borders. Although a few instances of self-organization by irregular migrants exist, these are not visible in the public sphere, and pro-regularization movements that exist in other European countries have not emerged in Germany (Laubenthal 2007b).

The German Residence Act on the duties of transmission of public institutions (Residence Act para. 87.2) is at the core of the German migration control system, and this has an important impact on the social rights of irregular migrants. All public institutions, schools and hospitals are obliged to inform the foreigners' office about the presence of an irregular migrant. Thus national law contains as a central element a provision that impedes irregular migrants' access to social rights. In 2007, the Federal Ministry of Interior re-stated that paragraph 87.2 of the Residence Act is 'a useful instrument of migration control that will not be subject to revisions' (Bundesministerium des Innern 2007). As a result, 'the lives and situations of non-nationals...without the necessary official documents are fundamentally characterized by their fear of discovery and sanction' (Schönwälder, Sciortino and Vogel 2006, p. 61).

Empirical studies stress that, because of the highly restrictive provisions of the migration control regime, irregular migrants try not to be noticed in their daily lives and avoid public places (Sinn, Kreienbrink and von Loeffeholz 2005, p. 62). While irregular migrants have a formal right to emergency health care, they often seek to cure health problems without professional medical care (ibid., p. 85). Regarding education, legal provisions that explicitly clarify irregular migrants' right to school attendance do not exist. However children must, on their enrolment in school, submit a certificate of residency showing that they have an official place of residence in Germany. It is assumed that the large majority of undocumented children do not attend school (Bommes and Wilmes 2007).

Civil society and irregular migrants' social rights

Instead, civil society activities play a central role in compensating for the restricted access of irregular migrants to social rights. Voluntary humanitarian organizations and local networks support irregular migrants in matters of health problems and the schooling of children. Local initiatives and welfare associations organize school attendance in informal ways, through private contacts with schools (Bommes and Wilmes 2007, p. 101), and networks of doctors and medical students provide health care (Sinn, Kreienbrink and von Loeffeholz 2005). While the degree of political activism by pro-immigration NGOs on the issue of irregular migration is comparatively low and political campaigns for a regularization of irregular migrants do not take place, since 2001 civil society actors and members of political parties have demanded better access to social rights for irregular migrants. A common feature of these claims is the use of human rights norms and international human rights agreements as a central argument for legitimating irregular migrants' access to social rights and for demanding the right of undocumented children to attend school.

At the federal level, important actors are churches and welfare organizations (Vogel and Assler 2010). Since 2001, the German Confederation of Bishops has often demanded the introduction of social rights minimum standards for irregular migrants, arguing that it 'wants … to remind [policy-makers] of the basic human rights orientation of the democratic German state' (Sekretariat der Deutschen Bischofskonferenz 2001). In 2007, a working group of the German bishops' conference reacted to the report of the Federal Ministry of the Interior that reiterated the applicability of Paragraph 87.2 Residence Act by stating that:

> The Catholic Forum demands to limit public institutions' obligation to transmit data about irregular migrants… .Federal state school laws must clarify that the residence status of children is irrelevant to their enrolment in school. The Catholic Forum demands the full ratification of the UN Convention on the Right of the Child without any reservations. (Katholisches Forum Leben in der Illegalität 2007)

In 2009 the welfare organization Caritas also demanded full access of irregular migrants to social rights, arguing that:

> human rights are the foundation of the state order. … Through several international treaties, Germany has committed itself to protect human rights. The enforcement of law and order clearly is a central task of the nation-state. However, if it does not want to

> undermine its own legitimacy, it must act on the basis of human rights. (Bundesarbeitsgemeinschaft der Freien Wohlfahrtspflege 2009)

Caritas further demanded the ratification of the UN Convention on the Rights of the Child without reservation (Bundesarbeitsgemeinschaft der Freien Wohlfahrtspflege 2009).

Political parties and irregular migrants' right to education

Educational rights for children of irregular migrants have become a topic of growing importance among political parties. In 2006, both the socialist party *Die Linke* and the Green Party submitted draft bills to the German parliament, demanding the 'unrestricted application of human rights in Germany' and the abolition of paragraph 87.2 of the Residence Act. Furthermore, both social-democratic and Christian-democratic politicians have made demands for the right of children without legal residence status to attend school. Thus the social-democratic spokesperson for the interior stated that 'we must urgently find ways to guarantee the right of education for irregular children. The UN Convention on the Rights of the Child...must be implemented' (*Der Spiegel* 7 April 2007). The chair of the Committee on Education of the German parliament stressed that irregular migrants have the 'same human right to education' as German pupils. The federal government and the federal states should enact regulations to this effect. She stated that this was a requirement of the UN Convention on the Rights of Children.[4] The Christian-democratic Federal Commissioner on Integration added: 'We need pragmatic regulations regarding the school attendance of undocumented children. The right to education is a human right' (*Süddeutsche Zeitung* 26 January 2009).

Federalism and the international human rights regime as an opportunity for migrants' social rights: the cases of Bavaria, North Rhine-Westphalia and Hesse

The importance of federal structures in migration policies has often been neglected by migration research. Research overwhelmingly focuses on national decision-making or on local approaches, implicitly assuming that the conditions within one nation-state are the same from region to region (Thränhardt 2001, p. 27): 'The institutional state structure of receiving countries and the relevance of the sub-national level has been widely neglected . . . although the majority of countries that have experienced immigration after 1945 are federally organized' (Henkes 2008, p. 114).

However, the potential impact of federal structures on migration policies in Germany has been addressed by Katzenstein (1987). Analysing the impact of the institutional configuration of the political system on policy change, he noted a generally low level of opportunities for policy change in the German case, due in part to the broad distribution of power between the federal and states' levels. Green's (2006) analysis of recent policy changes in the field of integration has confirmed the impact of these factors on the strong path-dependency of German migration policies. However, Thränhardt (2001) has highlighted the relevance of the sub-national level for differing policies in the field of migration. Because of the specific distribution of competencies, the central state has a higher influence on determining migration policies, such as the policies and the legal framework for the entry and stay of foreigners, while the sub-national level may have a significant influence on the establishment of differing integration policies. In particular, federal states' competences with respect to the implementation of integration policies contribute to the importance of the sub-national level.

More specific research that addresses the role of the regional level in German migration policies has shown the important role of the German federal states, i.e. the *Länder*, in citizenship policies. Despite consistent federal regulations on citizenship, significant differences exist among the German federal states regarding their naturalization quotas (Dornis 2001). Henkes (2008) has pointed out regional differences regarding the cultural dimensions of integration policies, such as differing regulations for allowing Muslim symbols in public institutions and on Muslim religious education in schools. Yet, while showing the importance of the German *Länder* as diverging actors in integration policies, these studies have focused exclusively on policies regarding migrants with legal residence status. They have not addressed the potential impact of federal structures on policies on irregular migration.

The issue of social rights for irregular migrants in Germany is structured partly by the German political system. The political order of the Federal Republic of Germany is to 'build from the federal states' (Wehling 2006, p. 7). German federalism is characterized by its joint decision-making (Scharpf, Reissert and Schnabel 1976; Scharpf 2006) but also by the strong influence of the federal states on national policy, based in part on their legislative veto right in the *Bundesrat*. The German *Länder* have a high degree of autonomy both regarding their institutional structure and in many policy fields (Hildebrandt and Wolf 2008, p. 11). Education represents the most important competence of the federal states (Wolf 2008, p. 21). The German constitution attributes both the regulation of access to education and regulation of compulsory school attendance to the federal states (Basic

Law Art. 70 ff.), with legislative competence on education devolved to the *Länder*. As a result, school structures, their educational principles and their spending on education differ widely among federal states (Wolf 2008, p. 21.).

Education is addressed both by the constitutions of the federal states and by the state's school laws. Regarding the question of school attendance of children without legal residence status, a tension arises from the fact that educational matters are the competence of the federal states, while the federal level intervenes by the law on the obligation of public institutions to transmit data about irregular migrants to the foreigners' office (Cyrus 2006, p. 3). Regulations regarding the access of irregular children differ from one federal state to another. While no school law explicitly addresses the issue, the school laws of Bavaria and North Rhine-Westphalia foresee compulsory school attendance for foreign minors who are obliged to leave the country (Sinn, Kreienbrink and von Loeffeholz 2005, p. 23). Against this background, in Bavaria, in North Rhine-Westphalia and in Hesse, local and regional administrations have enacted new regulations that aim to enable undocumented children to attend school.

Bavaria

The Bavarian school law, particularly its provision stating that school attendance is compulsory for foreign minors until their deportation, served as a framework for the Munich City Council to address the issue of educating undocumented migrants. Munich's traditionally left-wing city government represents an exception in the conservative state of Bavaria. In 2004, on the initiative of the Green Party, the city council commissioned a study on the living conditions of irregular migrants in Munich (Anderson 2003). It proposed that the city of Munich should clarify irregular migrants' right to education, recommending that schools should not control the residence status of foreign children.

Following the study's recommendations, the city council issued a declaration stating that there was no duty on schools to inform the foreigners' office about the presence of an irregular migrant either from the perspective of the school law or from the perspective of the foreigners' law. The council's central argument was that:

> Every person is protected by the human rights of the UN.... Germany has ratified a large body of other international and European treaties. The following decision is guided by these treaties....The right to education is a human right that must be protected. (Sozialreferat Stadt München 29 April 2004)

The city council requested school departments to inform all schools that school attendance was compulsory for irregular children. In this decree it stated that heads of schools were under no obligation to check the residence status of children attending their school.

North Rhine-Westphalia

In North Rhine-Westphalia, the liberal-conservative federal state government in 2007 enacted a new regulation concerning school attendance of irregular migrants. The regulation was based both on the federal state constitution declaring that 'every child is entitled to education ... school attendance is compulsory' and on the North Rhine-Westphalian school law, stating that:

> Every young person has, regardless of his economic situation, his origin or his gender a right to school education. ... School attendance is compulsory for everybody who is registered as a resident in North Rhine-Westphalia or who commonly lives in North Rhine-Westphalia. (School Law of North Rhine-Westphalia §34 1)

In 2008, the Ministry of Education in North Rhine-Westphalia issued a decree informing all schools that:

> School departments and schools have reported their uncertainty regarding their duty to transmit data on foreign children to the foreigners office, because of §87 Residence Act. Therefore, the Ministry of Education...declares that the Data Protection Ordinance on data of pupils and parents does not foresee the generation of data on the residence status of pupils. Schools may not ask for residence registrations of foreign pupils. If in single cases such data has been requested, this data has been unlawfully generated and must be destroyed. (Decree of the Ministry of Education 27 March 2008)

In an interview, a representative from the ministry stated that:

> This decree was made possible by the specific legal situation in North Rhine-Westphalia, and because of the existence of the data protection ordinance in the federal state law. Data protection regulation met human rights concerns. These people do not have the rights and duties of citizens, but they have human rights. (Interview, Ministry of Education of the Federal State of North Rhine-Westphalia, 31 July 2009)

The federal state of Hesse

Regulations on school attendance in Hesse are laid down in the federal state school law, stating that school attendance is compulsory for every child who has a place of residence in Hesse or who commonly lives in the federal state. The school attendance of migrant children is regulated by an additional decree, the 'Decree on school attendance of pupils of not-German mother tongue'. Before a reform of the decree on 1 January 2010, it requested foreign pupils to submit a certificate of residency when being enrolled at school (paragraph 4(2)). Debates and initiatives regarding the school attendance of children without a legal residence status started with the publication of an expert report on the issue of the right to education of irregular migrants (Interview, Ministry of Education of the Federal State of Hesse, 19 February 2010), commissioned by the trade union *Gewerkschaft Erziehung und Wissenschaft.*

The report stated that irregular children have a right to school attendance because of the Additional Protocol of the European Human Rights Convention and the German constitution. The debate on the report among the political parties in Hesse focused on the human rights aspects of the report, interpreting the decree on school attendance of pupils of not-German mother tongue provision's for a compulsory certificate of residence of irregular migrants as a violation of international human rights law (Interview, Ministry of Education of the Federal State of Hesse, 19 February 2010). The social-democratic, liberal and green parties argued for a reform of the school law that would enable children without legal residence status to attend school: 'The problem concerns many children who have been born and raised in Germany. They have a human right to education, too.'[5]

In 2009, the social-democratic party and the green party submitted a draft bill to the state parliament that aimed at changing the current school law and adopting the text of the school law of North Rhine-Westphalia.[6] In January 2010, the Hessian Ministry of Education issued a reformed version of the decree on school attendance of pupils of not-German mother tongue that abolished migrant pupils' need to submit a certificate of residence. The new regulation was welcomed by the social-democratic party whose spokesman stated: 'I am glad that the Ministry of Education regulation. . .contributes to the obligations of Art. 28 of the UN Convention on the Rights of the Child.'[7]

Conclusion

The German political context regarding irregular migration is characterized by several important factors that counteract irregular migrants' access to social rights. While irregular migrants formally have the right to emergency health care and no legal provisions exist that explicitly deny the right of migrants without legal residence status to attend school, the restrictive national migration control regime with its highly developed system of surveillance and internal controls strongly discourages migrants' access to public institutions. Furthermore, national migration control law explicitly aims at preventing migrants' access to social rights by obliging all public institutions to report the stay of a foreigner without legal residence status. Civil societies' activities in the field of irregular migration are largely characterized by a humanitarian approach, providing irregular migrants with voluntarily organized health care and support in enrolling children at school through informal networks. While generally the degree of politicization of irregular migration in the public sphere is low and political mobilizations of irregular migrants do not exist, humanitarian networks, churches and welfare organizations lobby for better access of irregular migrants to social rights. A central framing element of their claims is the existence of the international human rights regime.

Against this background, the specific institutional structure of the German political system has provided opportunities for policy changes in the field of irregular migrants' social rights. While one central feature of German federalism, namely its cooperative structure and the joint decision-making process of the national level and the *Länder*, generally leads to few opportunities for policy change on migration, another characteristic of German federalism – the high degree of autonomy of the federal states in the field of education – has provided an opportunity for policy change regarding irregular migrants' social rights. Education as a core competence of the federal states, reflected in their strongly differing education policies and regionally differing laws on education, has encouraged the introduction of new regulations that aim at enforcing irregular migrants' right to education. Policy changes have happened in two ways: federal state governments themselves have initiated policy changes and local level authorities have used the federal structure of the German political system in order to grant social rights to irregular migrants. In particular, policy changes to enable children without legal residence status to attend school have taken place through administrative procedures and interpretations of regional legal and administrative regulations.

In all cases, the granting of social rights for migrants was enacted by provisions that challenge direct or indirect provisions of the national migration control regime. In Bavaria and North Rhine-Westphalia, regulations were introduced that exempt schools from complying with the provisions of the national Residence Act that obliges public institutions to inform the foreigners' office about an irregular stay. In North Rhine-Westphalia, existing federal state laws on data protection were used as an instrument in this process. In the federal state of Hesse, school attendance of children without legal residence status was encouraged by a regulation counteracting the indirect negative effects by the national migration control regime on the right to education, specifically the obligation of foreign pupils to prove officially that they have a place of residence in Germany.

The international human rights regime served as a central frame for legitimating policy changes on irregular migrants' right to education. The focus on human rights in the discourses that accompanied the introduction of new regulations on education in several German federal states highlights the discursive power of the international human rights regime in encouraging policy change in the field of irregular migration, regardless of the actual material implementation of international human rights treaties in national law. The public negotiation of educational rights of irregular migrants in Germany shows that, although on issues such as naturalization and migration law significant differences among parties exist, human rights as a discursive instrument transcend political orientations and party cleavages, While in the case of Munich, a left-wing coalition issued new regulations on irregular migrants' right to attend school, in the Federal States of Hesse and North Rhine-Westphalia liberal-conservative governments enacted the policy changes. Also, at the federal level, politicians of all political parties present in the German parliament made demands for educational rights for irregular migrants, based on the existence of international human rights norms.

The new regional regulations on the educational rights of irregular migrants that have been enacted with the discursive support of the international human rights regime represent a significant change in the German political approach to irregular migration. In particular, they contain a change in the overarching terms of policy discourse (Hall 1993, p. 279) on irregular migration. Furthermore, they counteract the central aims and policy instruments of the national migration control regime. As part of the process of granting new social rights to irregular migrants, German national sovereignty in the field of migration has been challenged from both the international and the sub-national level. The implementation of new policies on irregular migration in Germany shows the importance of the regional level in migration policies, and it highlights the need for further research on the relationship between the institutional structure of a nation-state and its migration policies.

Acknowledgements

I would like to thank the three anonymous reviewers of Ethnic and Racial Studies, Lesley Wexler and Gerard Boucher for their very helpful comments on earlier drafts of this article.

Notes

1. Irregular migration here is understood as 'immigration of persons who do not or not any more fulfil legal requirements of entry and stay' (Vogel and Assler 2010, p. 6).
2. Universal Declaration of Human Rights (1948); International Convention on the Elimination of all Forms of Racial Discrimination (1965); International Covenant on Civil and Political Rights (1966); International Covenant on Economic, Social and Cultural Rights (1966); Convention on the Elimination of All Forms of Discrimination against Women (1979); International Convention on the Protection of the Rights of All Migrant Workers and their Families (1990); Convention on the Rights of the Child (1990).
3. United Nations Treaty Collection, Ddatabase, consulted 2 October 2010.
4. http://www.focus.de/schule/schule/recht/recht-auf-bildung-schulbesuch-fuer-alle-illegalen-kinder_aid_361520.html (accessed 22 February 2010).
5. http://www.migazin.de/2009/07/08/Hesse-kein-schulbesuch-fur-illegale-kinder-im-schulj ahr-20092010 (accessed 22 February 2010).
6. http://www.migazin.de/2009/07/09/Hesse-spd-und-grune-lassen-kinder-ohne-aufenthalts status-nicht-im-stich (22 February 2010).
7. http://www.migazin.de/2009/10/02/landesregierung-regelt-schulbesuch-von-statuslosen-kindern (accessed 22 February 2010).

References

ANDERSON, P. 2003 *Dass sie uns nicht vergessen: Eine empirische Studie im Auftrag der Landeshauptstadt München*, München: Landeshauptstadt München. Sozialreferat

BIELEFELD, H. 2006 'Menschenrechte "irregulärer" Migrantinnen und Migranten', in Jörg Alt and Michael Bommes (eds), *Illegalität: Grenzen und Möglichkeiten der Migrationspolitik*, Wiesbaden: VS-Verlag, pp. 81–93

BOGUSZ, B. C., RYSZARD, CHOLEWINSKI, CYCAN, ADAM and SZYSZCZAK, ERIKA 2004 *Irregular Migration and Human Rights: Theoretical, European and International Perspectives*, Leiden: Martinus Nijhoff

BOMMES, M. 2006 'Illegale Migration in der modernen Gesellschaft: Resultat und Problem der Migrationspolitik europäischer Nationalstaaten', in Jörg Alt and Michael Bommes (eds), *Illegalität: Grenzen und Möglichkeiten der Migrationspolitik*, Wiesbaden: VS-Verlag, pp. 95–116

BOMMES, M. and WILMES, M. 2007 *Menschen ohne Papiere in Köln: Eine Studie zur Lebenssituation irregulärer Migranten*, Osnabrück: Institut für Migrationsforschung und Interkulturelle Studien

BUNDESARBEITSGEMEINSCHAFT DER FREIEN WOHLFAHRTSPFLEGE (2009) Positionspapier der Bundesarbeitsgemeinschaft der Freien Wohlfahrtspflege Menschen in der aufenthaltsrechtlichen Illegalität in Deutschland. December 2009

BUNDESMINISTERIUM DES INNEREN (2007) Illegal aufhältige Migranten in Deutschland. Datenlage, Rechtslage, Handlungsoptionen. Bericht des Bundesministeriums des Innern zum Prüfauftrag "Illegalität" aus der Koalitionsvereinbarung vom 11. November 2005, Kapitel VIII 1.2, Februar 2007. Berlin: Bundesministerium des Inneren

CHOLEWINSKI, R. 1997 *Migrant Workers in International Human Rights Law: Their Protection in Countries of Employment*, Oxford: Clarendon Press

——— 2006 *Irregular Migrants: Access to Minimum Social Rights*, Strasbourg: Council of Europe

CREMER, H. 2009 *Das Recht auf Bildung für Kinder ohne Papiere: Empfehlungen zur Umsetzung*, Policy Paper No. 14, Deutsches Institut für Menschenrechte

CYRUS, N. 2006 'Stellungnahme zur öffentlichen Anhörung des Innenausschusses des Deutschen Bundestages zum Gesetzesentwurf der Abegordneten Joseph Philip Winkler und der Fraktion Bündnis 90/Die Grünen "Entwurf eines Gesetzes zur Verbesserung der sozialen

Situation von Ausländerinnen und Ausländern, die ohne Aufenthaltstitel in Deutschland leben (BT-Drucksache 16/445)"'
——— 2008 *Undocumented Migration: Counting the uncountable: Data and Trends across Europe: CLANDESTINO Country report Germany*
DEUTSCHE BISCHOFSKONFERENZ (2001) Leben in der Illegalität in Deutschland – eine humanitäre und pastorale Herausforderung. 21. Mai 2001. Bonn: Sekretariat der Deutschen Bischofskonferenz
DORNIS, C. 2001 'Einbürgerung in Deutschland: Die Verwaltungspraxis in verschiedenen Regionen im Vergleich', in Dietrich Thränhardt (ed.), *Integrationspolitik in föderalistischen Systemen*, Münster: Lit-Verlag, pp. 63–90
DÜVELL, F. 2006 'Auch "Illegale" haben Rechte: Schutz von Sans-Papiers im europäischen Vergleich', in *Tagung 'Soziale Rechte von Menschen ohne Aufenthaltsstatus'*, Schmitten: Evangelische Akademie Arnoldshain
GEDDIE, E. and LEVOY, M. 2009 *PICUM's Main Concerns about the Fundamental Rights of Undocumented Migrants in Europe 2009.* Brussels: PICUM
GLORIUS, B. 2006 'Country report Germany', in Jeroen Doomernik and Michael Jandl (eds), *Modes of Migration Control and Regulation in Europe*, Amsterdam: Amsterdam University Press, pp. 81–104
GREEN, S. 2006 'Zwischen Kontinuität und Wandel: Migrations- und Staatsangehörigkeitspolitik', in Manfred Schmidt and Reimut Zohlnhöfer (eds), *Regieren in der Bundesrepublik Deutschland: Innen- und Aussenpolitik seit 1949*, Wiesbaden: VS-Verlag, pp. 113–34
HALL, P. 1993 'Policy paradigms, social learning and the state: the case of economic policy-making in Britain', *Comparative Politics*, vol. 25, no. 3, pp. 275–96
HANSEN, R. 2002 'Globalization, embedded realism, and path dependence: the other immigrants to Europe', *Comparative Political Studies*, vol. 35, no. 3, pp. 259–83
HENKES, C. 2008 'Integrationspolitik in den Bundesländern', in Achim Hildebrandt and Frieder Wolf (eds), *Die Politik der Bundesländer: Staatstätigkeit im Vergleich*, Wiesbaden: VS Verlag für Sozialwissenschaften, pp. 113–35
HILDEBRANDT, A. and WOLF, F. 2008 *Die Politik der Bundesländer: Staatstätigkeit im Vergleich*, Wiesbaden: VS Verlag für Sozialwissenschaften
KATHOLISCHES FORUM "LEBEN IN DER ILLEGALITÄT" (2007) Stellungnahme Zum Bericht des Bundesministeriums des Innern zum Prüfauftrag "Illegalität" aus der Koalitionsvereinbarung vom 11. November 2005, Kapitel VIII 1.2 Illegal aufhältige Migranten in Deutschland – Datenlage, Rechtslage, Handlungsoptionen, Februar 2007
KATZENSTEIN, P. J. 1987 *Policy and Politics in West Germany: The Growth of a Semi-Sovereign State*, Philadelphia, PA: Temple University Press
KOSER, K. 2005 'Irregular migration, state security and human security', paper prepared for the policy analysis and research programme of the Global Commission for International Migration, September
LAUBENTHAL, B. 2007a *Der Kampf um Legalisierung: Soziale Bewegungen illegaler Migranten in Frankreich, Spanien und der Schweiz*, Frankfurt am Main: Campus-Verlag
——— 2007b 'The emergence of pro-regularization movements in Western Europe', *International Migration*, vol. 45, no. 3, pp. 101–33
LAUBENTHAL, B. and NIELAND, J.-U. 2007 'Migration policy in Germany: do the media matter?', Public Policy and the Mass Media, paper presented to the Workshop of the ECPR, Helsinki
MÉDECINS DU MONDE EUROPEAN OBSERVATORY ON HEALTHCARE 2009 *Access to Health Care for Undocumented Migrants in Eleven European Countries: 2008 Survey Report*
PECOUD, A. and DE GUCHTENEIRE, P. 2004 'Migration, human rights and the United Nations: an investigation into the low ratification record of the UN migrant workers convention', *Global Migration Perspectives* 3, Geneva: Global Commission on International Migration

PICUM 2008 *Undocumented Children in Europe: Victims of Immigration Restrictions*, Brussels: PICUM

——— 2009 'Clandestino: understanding irregular migration in Northern Europe', Workshop, London, 27 March

SCHABAS, W. 'Reservations to the Convention on the Rights of the Child', *Human Rights Quarterly*, vol. 18, no. 2, pp. 472–91

SCHARPF, F. 2006 'The Joint-decision trap revisited', *Journal of Common Market Studies*, vol. 44, no. 4, pp. 845–64

SCHARPF, F., REISSERT, B. and SCHNABEL, F. 1976 *Politikverflechtung: Theorie und Empirie des kooperativen Föderalismus in der Bundesrepublik*, Kronberg/Ts.: Scriptor

SCHÖNWÄLDER, K., SCIORTINO, G. and VOGEL, D. 2006 'Migration and illegality in Germany', *AKI Research Review 1*, Berlin

SCIORTINO, G. 2004 'Between phantoms and necessary evils: some critical points in the study of irregular migrations to Western Europe', *IMIS-Beiträge*, no. 24, pp. 17–43

SINN, A., KREIENBRINK, A. and VON LOEFFEHOLZ, H. D. 2005 *Illegally Resident Third-Country Nationals in Germany: Policy Approaches, Profile and Social Situation: Research Study within the Framework of the European Migration Network*, Nürnberg: BAMF

THRÄNHARDT, D. 2001 'Zuwanderungs- und Integrationspolitik in föderalistischen Ländern', in Dietrich Thränhardt (ed.), *Integrationspolitik in föderalistischen Ländern*, Münster: Lit-Verlag, pp. 15–34

VOGEL, D. 2009a 'How many irregular residents are there in Germany? Estimates on the basis of police criminal statistics', *Database on Irregular Migration, Working Paper No.3*, Hamburg Institute of International Economics

——— 2009b *Illegalität von Kindern in Deutschland: Plausibilitätsüberlegungen und Alternativberechnungen zur Zahl der Kinder ohne Aufenthaltsstatus*, Hamburg: Hamburgisches Weltwirtschaftsinstitut

VOGEL, D. and ASSNER, M. 2010 *Kinder ohne Aufenthaltsstatus – illegal im Land, legal in der Schule: Studie für den Sachverständigenrat deutscher Stiftungen für Integration und Migration*, Berlin, http://irregular-migration.hwwi.de/Germany-Link-librar.6141.0.html

VOGEL, D. and CYRUS, N. 2008 *Irregular Migration in Europe: Doubts about the Effectiveness of Control Strategies*. Focus Migration Policy Brief No. 9

WEHLING, H.-G. 2006 'Landespolitik und Länderpolitik im föderalistischen System Deutschlands', in Herbert Schneider and Hans-Georg Wehling (eds), *Landespolitik in Deutschland: Grundlagen-Strukturen-Arbeitsfelder*, Wiesbaden: VS Verlag für Sozialwissenschaften, pp. 7–21

WEXLER, L. 2007 'The non-legal role of human rights law in addressing immigration', in *University of Chicago Legal Forum 439 (symposium)*

WOLF, F. 2008 'Die Schulpolitik: Kernbestand der Kulturhoheit', in Hildebrandt Achim and Wolf Frieder (eds), *Die Politik der Bundesländer*, Wiesbaden: VS Verlag für Sozialwissenschaften, pp. 22–41

Social effects of mass deportations by the United States government, 2000–10

Jacqueline Maria Hagan, Nestor Rodriguez and Brianna Castro

Abstract

Interviews with deportees in El Salvador and Mexico and with immigrants in the United States indicate that expanded US enforcement policies are straining transnational families and imposing fear on immigrant communities. Expanded enforcement is removing long-term settlers with strong kinship ties to the United States. Through various strategies, some immigrants attempt to cope with new enforcement operations, while others involuntarily return to their home communities. The findings suggest that (1) conceptualizations of immigration policy enactment of the 'liberal state' need to be reassessed, and (2) migration policies of the United States, Mexico and El Salvador need to be revisited in light of their human costs.

Introduction

The United States has a long history of mass deportations of foreign-born persons. Although we can trace the hardening of the US deportation system back to the Chinese Exclusion Act of 1882, three mass deportations have occurred since World War I. The first occurred during the Great Depression when Mexicans became the targets of America's economic troubles, leading to the repatriation of over 400,000 Mexican migrants (Hoffman 1974). The second mass deportation occurred in 1954 when the US government removed over one million Mexican migrants through 'Operation Wetback' (Lytle Hernandez 2006; US Department of Homeland Security 2010, table 36). Since the mid-1990s, changes in immigration policy and deportation law have ushered in a third period of mass deportation, one that like its predecessors affects mainly Latinos. More than 350,000 immigrants now face formal deportation proceedings each year. What distinguishes the present era of mass deportation from earlier ones is the presence of a vast state technology that enables the melding of two different methods of deportation: extended border control and interior social control (Kanstroom 2007).

Responding to the rise in deportation in recent years, scholars have begun discussing how liberal democracies use deportation to regulate immigration. Mathew Gibney and Randall Hansen (2003) argue that deportation embodies what they term the 'liberal democratic paradox'. On the one hand, fundamental to the sovereignty of the state is the capacity to control borders. On the other hand, immigration must also reflect the rights of its residents. The conflict between support for sovereignty and rights bears on the course of deportation policy. Antje Ellermann (2009), Rachel Ida Buff (2008) and Lisa Flores (2003) identify political actors and conditions that have historically produced different patterns of coercive social regulation. Flores documents the ways in which anti-immigrant sentiment and US deportation programmes have followed periods of racialized portrayals of immigrants. Buff argues that the growing and vast state technology, which includes multiple entities charged with immigration control, has produced an operation of deportation terror. Daniel Kanstroom (2007) introduces the concept of 'post-entry social control' and explains increased deportations in the interior United States as a function of failed control of the border.

Although this scholarship informs our research, the primary purpose of our paper is not to extend the theoretical and legal discussions of deportation, but to examine the implications of changes in immigration policy and deportation law for those they target – immigrants. Drawing on research in Mexico, El Salvador and the United States, we ask: (1) How has the expansion of US immigration enforcement policy into the interior United States affected the characteristics of immigrant populations at risk for deportation? (2) What are the implications of enforcement changes for deportees, immigrants and their families? and (3) What strategies have immigrants developed to navigate enforcement operations?

Contemporary deportation policy

Present-day deportations result from a series of laws that elevate exterior border control and interior social control (Kanstroom 2007). The 1996 Illegal Immigration Reform and Immigrant Responsibility Act (IIRIRA) was the first of the laws enacted since the mid-1990s that increased deportations by increasing the offences for which an immigrant could be deported, by expanding the categories of noncitizens eligible for deportation and by restricting the ability of migrants to appeal deportation (Aleinkoff, Martin and Motomura 2001).

The Antiterrorism and Effective Death Penalty Act (AEDPA) of 1996 further increased the enforcement authority of the federal government by almost eliminating judicial review for most categories of immigrants subject to deportation. By weakening judicial review, AEDPA removed the legal constraints that protected noncitizens from deportation and thus eliminated relief for noncitizens with family ties in the United States (Kanstroom 2007).

In 2001, Congress passed the USA PATRIOT Act, which bolstered administrative authority to apprehend, detain and deport immigrants who are perceived to be threats to national security (Salter 2004). In 2003, the newly created Department of Homeland Security (DHS) streamlined the previous immigration and border control responsibilities of the Immigration and Naturalization Service, elevating government capacity and authority to carry out federal policies and programmes, including Endgame, a strategic plan devised in 2003 with the goal of removing all deportable migrants by 2012 (DHS 2003).

In 2003, DHS created the Bureau of Immigration and Customs Enforcement (ICE), a new agency dedicated to apprehending, detaining and deporting 'criminal and fugitive' noncitizens long after their arrival (Kanstroom 2007). ICE has launched a series of programmes in which they collaborate with state and local agencies. The Criminal Alien Program (CAP) places ICE officials at state prisons to conduct immigrant screening. The Secure Communities Program relies on police to enter prints of arrestees into a joint FBI and ICE database. Currently implemented in over 1000 counties in thirty-eight states, the programme's goals include nationwide implementation by 2013. The most controversial enforcement initiative is the 287(g) programme, which trains state and local police to identify, process and detain suspect immigrants whom they encounter during their regular law-enforcement activities. The programme has trained and certified over 1000 officers from seventy-two jurisdictions (Capps *et al.* 2011).

The recoding of civil violations into criminal acts and expansion of enforcement operations from the border to a vast state technology of federal and local enforcement agencies in the interior United States has led to the current period of mass deportations. Figure 1 shows that since the mid-1990s deportations have surged: from 1996 through 2005, yearly removals averaged around 180,000; from 2006 through 2009 they increased further, reaching 393,289 in 2009 (DHS 2010, table 36). Most recent removals from the United States are non-criminal immigrants from Mexico and Central America. In FY 2009, 72 per cent of those deported were from Mexico and 20 per cent from

Figure 1 *Deportations from the United States, 1900–2008*

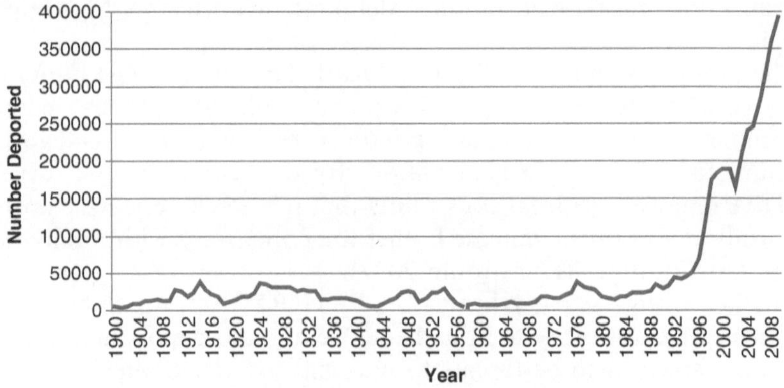

Source*: US Department of Homeland Security (2008)Security (2009)*

Central America, and only 33 per cent of the total deported were removed for criminal violations (DHS 2010, table 38).

Research on the apprehension, detention and deportation of immigrants

Although ICE argues that US interior enforcement policy is developed to capture criminals, studies consistently find that interior enforcement operations do not target serious offenders as intended by deportation law. Many immigrants are arrested without warrants by local police solely because they are status violators or have committed minor violations such as speeding or driving without a license (US Government Accounting Office 2009; Weissman, Headen and Lewis Parker 2009; Capps *et al.* 2011).

Studies also report a lack of federal oversight of local enforcement policies (Capps *et al.* 2011). Consequently, the implementation and effects of local enforcement initiatives like 287(g) vary widely. In some communities enforcement operations open the door to racial profiling and unlawful arrest responses and practices (Southern Poverty Law Center 2009; Weissman, Headen and Lewis Parker 2009; Capps *et al.* 2011). Phillips, Hagan and Rodriguez (2006), for example, found that in some jurisdictions deportees were subjected to excessive force during arrest (compared with the arrest of citizens), as well as to demeaning racial slurs during arrest and detention. Moreover, deportees reported more use of excessive force when arrested by local police than by US immigration officials, a finding that raises serious questions about local police involvement in immigration enforcement. Variations in local enforcement effects are also driven by local concerns that are shaped by political pressures (Buff 2008; Capps *et al.* 2011). In some new destination communities in the southeast and southwest, the rapid growth of Latino immigrants has fuelled anti-immigrant sentiment and placed pressure on local police to enforce immigration law with a hard hand (Capps *et al.* 2011).

The conditions under which immigrants are detained after arrest may also fall short of US and international standards. Detainees spend long periods in detention facilities and are often subject to racial slurs and excessive force (Phillips, Hagan and Rodriguez. 2006). Findings by Amnesty International (2009) and the investigative arm of DHS, the Office of the Inspector General (DHS 2006), included instances of mistreatment and neglect of immigrant detainees, such as inadequate health care, noncompliance with detention confinement guidelines and lack of a process for detainees to report abuses or civil rights violations.

Fear of deportation and distrust of local officials permeates Latino communities in the United States. Businesses, faith groups, local officials, school officials and even local law enforcement have expressed concern over the local enforcement practices. Facing the possibility of deportation, migrants have shied away from public places, churches, schools and health services, and social service staff confirm declines in client participation (Rodriguez and Hagan 2044; Capps et al. 2011). In Houston, some Latinos who regularly relied on a mobile health clinic van for health services changed their reported identities from 'Hispanic' to 'White' to avoid detection (Rodriguez and Hagan 2004). In their seven-county study of interior enforcement effects, Capps *et al.* (2011) found that immigrants moved from jurisdictions with 287(g) to neighbouring jurisdictions that had not implemented 287(g), and that Hispanic public school enrollment figures dropped (followed by rebounds) in some 287(g) counties as migrants left and as roadblocks and other operations increased (Capps *et al.* 2011).

Deportation also has social and psychological effects on families. Using census data and figures released by the Pew Hispanic Center, a recent Human Rights Watch report (2009) estimates that more than one million family members have been separated from one another through deportation. Many are long-term settlers whose deportation has dramatic effects on their families, disrupting relationships, remittances and settlement behaviour. Hagan, Eschbach and Rodriguez (2008) found that deportees leave behind spouses or children in the United States, many of whom are US-born children. Deportation produces emotional and psychological hardship for deportees and traumatic effects among children and spouses left behind (Capps *et al.* 2007; Mendoza and Olivas 2009). Not surprisingly, social ties to spouses and children remaining in the United States increase the likelihood that deportees will plan to migrate again (Hagan, Eschbach and Rodriguez 2008).

Methodological approach, research sites and samples

To examine the impact of expanded enforcement activities on immigrants, we first rely on two surveys conducted with deported migrants in El Salvador in 2002 and 2008. We also draw on two field studies, one of which included fifty in-depth interviews conducted in 2008 and 2009 with immigrants and community and leaders in Johnston County, North Carolina; the other included in-depth interviews with return migrants in 2010 in Mexico.

All persons deported from the United States to El Salvador arrive at one airport and participate in a reception programme called *Bienvenido a Casa* (BAC) or 'Welcome Home'. BAC was established in 1998 with the support of Catholic Relief Services (CRS), the International Organization for Migration (IOM) and the US Department of State. From 1998 through most of 2004, BAC kept a brief, ongoing census of all deportees. In early 2002 the director of BAC expressed interest in a study that would examine conditions of exit and the consequences of deportation for deportees and their US and Salvadoran families. In 2002, 300 interviews were conducted with a random sample of deportees. These interviews comprise the 2002 deportee sample in Table 1.

In summer 2008, one of the authors travelled to El Salvador to investigate the viability of doing a follow-up study of a sub-sample of the deportees interviewed in 2002. By this time, BAC had been transferred to El Salvador's Ministry of Migration and Foreign Affairs and, in its charge, the programme's mission had been transformed from a reintegration to a regulatory role aimed at monitoring the deportee population. Access to BAC records was denied, but the author was granted access to the most recent BAC census (2008) and, under government supervision, was permitted to interview fifty-nine recently arrived deportees. These interviews constitute the 2008 deportee sample in Table 1.

To investigate how deportees, immigrants, their families and the US have been affected by expanded enforcement and changes in deportation law, we also draw on two field studies. The first took place in North Carolina, a state that until the late 1980s had little experience with Latinos. As a new destination, its Latino population grew by 394 per cent between 1990 and 2000, reaching 378,963 by the end of the decade. In 2010, it comprised 7.7 per cent of the state's population (US Census Bureau 2010). Among the states with counties that have submitted requests to partner with ICE through the 287(g) programme, North Carolina is the most heavily represented; twenty-two

Table 1. *Deportee samples and BAC censuses, 2002 and 2008*

	Deportee samples %		BAC deportee censuses %*	
	2002	2008	2002	2008
Gender				
Male	95	81	95	81
Female	5	19	5	19
Age				
18–30	56	36	59	Na**
31–40	27	20	29	Na
Over 40	16	10	12	Na
Not reported	1	34		
Years in the United States				
0 to 5	43	92	50	Na
6 to 10	16	3	20	Na
More than 10	38	5	30	Na
Not reported	4			
Reason for deportation				
Immigration violation	56	27	64	68
Crime (not immigration)	43	NR	36	32
Not reported	2	73		
Number of deportees in sample	300	59	10,876	20,302

*Data for 2002 census was obtained from Catholic Relief Services (2002), and data for the 2008 census was obtained from EI Salvador Ministerio de Justicia y Seguridad Publica (2009).

**These data were unavailable because the census included fewer categories of information.

of the state's counties have applied to become 287(g) partners. In 2007, 3,100 immigrants in North Carolina were placed in proceedings through 287(g) (Niolet 2008; Weissman, Headen and Lewis Parker 2009). Our study site is Johnston County, North Carolina, a largely rural county, that is home to a diverse Latino population of newcomer and established Mexicans, Central and South Americans.

In fall 2008 and spring 2009, one author (Castro) interviewed fifty Latino undocumented and legal residents in Johnston County. In fall 2009, the author returned to Johnston County to re-interview immigrants and community members to assess how conditions had changed over a year of expanded local enforcement.

In Mexico, our research takes place in Guanajuato, the central Mexican state with a long history of migration and return migration to and from the United States and, more recently, to and from North Carolina. In summer 2010, one author (Hagan) completed interviews with a random sample of 200 recent return migrants, one fourth of whom were recent deportees. Several narratives from these interviews are presented in this paper.

The changing profile of those deported from the United States

The extension of enforcement into the interior of the United States has expanded the immigrant population at risk of deportation. We can see this transformation by comparing the 2002 deportee sample with the 2008 sample on four characteristics: sex, age, time in the United States and reason reported for deportation.

As Table 1 shows, the deportees in both study samples and BAC censuses are overwhelmingly young and male, a finding that is consistent with the selective nature of undocumented migration. On the other hand, although the large majority of deportees are men, the table shows that the percentage of females in both the study samples and BAC censuses more than tripled from 2002 to 2008, from five to nineteen per cent. This increase is suggestive of a shift from border to interior enforcement. Prior to the creation of ICE in 2003, enforcement operations were primarily concentrated at points of entry, with occasional random raids at locations where males dominate, such as labour pools and large job sites. With the implementation of interior enforcement activities in immigrant communities, an increasing number of women and mothers are now at risk of deportation.

Deportees varied in the length of time they had resided in the United States. A substantial portion interviewed in 2002 and especially in 2008 were recent arrivals. In both study samples, and in the BAC 2002 census, most deportees who reported living in the United States for less than five years had been deported on the day of their arrival at a port of entry. Nonetheless, over a third of the 2002 study sample and almost a third of the 2002 BAC census reported living in the United States for more than ten years.

The effects of enforcement activities in the US interior are reflected in the reported reasons for deportation given in Table 1. The percentage of deportees who reported in the BAC censuses that they were deported for immigration violations increased from 2002 to 2008. This trend does not appear in the 2008 study sample due to a high level of non-reporting and the reluctance of deportees to report a criminal reason for deportation in the presence of Salvadoran state officials. The data reported by the DHS demonstrate this similar trend. As Figure 2 shows, since 2003, when ICE commenced its interior enforcement campaigns, the number of non-criminal removals has increased dramatically.

Figure 2 *Removals to El Salvador by reasons for removal*

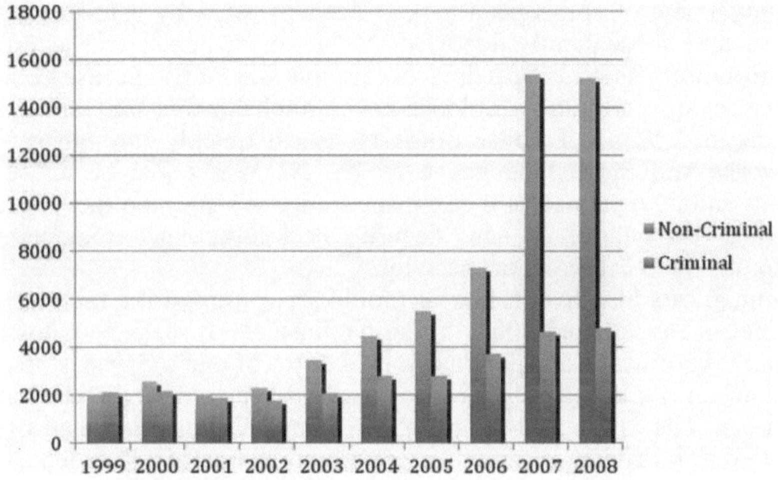

Source: *US Department of Homeland Security (2009)*

Social effects of interior social control and immigrant responses

Established immigrant families living in the interior United States now live in fear as local police implement new control measures in the everyday spaces and activities of immigrant communities. Local law enforcement in immigration matters has been especially pronounced in new destination states like North Carolina and in small rural areas, like Johnston County, where established residents are less tolerant of newcomers than their urban counterparts (Bada *et al.* 2010). The racialization and criminalization of Latino immigrants by Johnston County officials has fuelled anti-immigrant sentiment among local residents, who voice their support for local police involvement on several blog sites. The local sheriff, Steve Bizzell, is a strong advocate of local immigration enforcement. As chairman of the state's Sheriff Association, Bizzell helped to make North Carolina the first state to partner with ICE in deportation proceedings. Bizzell has vocalized his hostility towards Mexican immigrants, calling them 'trashy' and 'breeders'. He blames newcomers for crime in the county and state, although this argument has been debunked by a study that finds that crime rates have actually decreased in North Carolina counties where immigration had increased (Nguyen and Gill 2010).

Traffic stops have become the new enforcement strategy in Johnston County and immigrants live in fear. Undocumented migrants drive in fear because they cannot obtain a driver's license without a valid Social Security number. Respondents reported that they are regularly profiled, followed by police and pulled over for no apparent reason.

More than three-quarters of the fifty persons interviewed in Johnston County knew of someone who had been arrested by a local police officer and subsequently deported. Most were stopped and arrested for violations such as speeding or driving without a license. Local police set up periodic roadblocks near establishments frequented by immigrants. Word of police dragnets spread quickly through social networks and Spanish language media. As Maria, the owner of a beauty salon, explained, 'I'll be cutting someone's hair and they'll get a warning call about a new license checkpoint and immediately announce it to everyone in the salon.'

Immigrants also live in fear of family separation. Take the case of Veronica. In summer 2008, a Latina business owner in Johnston County, Veronica, was approached by a sister of one of her customers with an unusual request. The sister had a 9-year-old boy and a baby with her. The mother of the children, Veronica's customer, had been arrested for driving without a license and deported. The deported woman was a single mother and her children were left with her sister who was unable to care for them, since she was unemployed and living with a friend. Veronica felt she had to do something. She decided to take in the 9-year-old boy but not the 6-month-old baby. As she explained, 'I can't keep an infant in the restaurant and there is no one at home to care for it. The boy still lives with me but he is sad, shy, and regularly cries for his mother and baby brother'. His mother has not been able to get back to the States.

How have newcomers and established immigrants, long-term residents and community leaders in Johnston County responded to expanded enforcement? What strategies, if any, have immigrants developed to circumvent enforcement operations in the course of their everyday lives? How effective are these strategies?

As in other communities in the southeastern United States composed primarily of blacks and whites and with little history of immigration, Latino immigrants in Johnston County do not have an established political source to turn to for advocacy on their behalf. But in the wake of the May Day immigrant marches of 2006, the civic engagement and political participation of Latinos throughout the country increased and many alliances and coalitions were formed between Latino immigrants and other established elements of civil society, including business associations, immigrant advocacy networks and political leaders (Bada *et al.* 2010).

In Johnston County, the foreign and native-born Latino community founded a chapter of Yes We Can, an organization dedicated to immigration reform. At bi-monthly town meetings, the president of the coalition, an established Latino resident, presents the concerns of Latino immigrants, faith groups and business owners. Alliances of business leaders, faith workers and concerned citizens regularly meet at a local church to assess the effects of 287(g) on their community. These meetings, organized by academics from the local community college, are geared towards discussing the social and economic costs of the 287(g) programme.

Informal alliances have also developed between legal and undocumented migrants in the community. Groups of legal Latino residents respond to the 287(g) programme by assisting undocumented migrants. As Juan, a long-term resident and Honduran immigrant, explained:

> One way we help each other is that when someone is picked up by police, all of their friends will gather money for bail. When we have enough money, someone in the community with documents takes the money to the jail and bails out our friend as soon as possible.

The Latino community in Johnston County knows that ICE vans come to the jail only one day a week to take into custody and subsequently deport undocumented immigrants. Juan pointed out, ‘We’ve learned that immigration agents come to the jail on Tuesdays to search for undocumented immigrants; if we can get our friend out of jail before ICE arrives they will not be detected by immigration.’

Legal residents also help their undocumented counterparts with daily necessities. Most employers in Johnston County have begun asking potential employees for proof of legal residence, resulting in more unemployed migrant workers. Without drivers’ licenses and with undocumented status, many immigrants in the area are unable to access social services, including food stamps for their US-born children. Legal immigrants have stepped in to assist these migrants by locating food banks as far away as Raleigh and driving those in need to pick up food items each week.

The fear of driving without a license has become so severe that people with licenses have started driving unlicensed Latinos to work. Posted on bulletin boards in many Latino businesses across Johnston County are Spanish flyers advertising transportation assistance to and from work. A legal resident, Josefina, comments, ‘We give each other rides to work, the doctor, the grocery store, that’s just the way we live here.’ Others, under the guidance and companionship of a legal resident and/or citizen, have travelled to states that still provide drivers licensed to undocumented migrants.

Religion is central in the lives of Latino immigrants, and religious institutions have historically played a central role in protecting the rights of migrants. In an era of mass deportations, the public face of the Catholic Church has been especially visible; it was a leading organizer behind the 2006 marches, and continues to play a strong role in advocating national immigration reform (Hagan 2008). As the single most trusted institution for many Latinos, the Catholic Church plays an important role in mitigating community policing. In Johnston County, the local Catholic Church provides space for Latino organizations and disseminates information to the larger Latino community informing immigrants about their rights. Each Sunday at the end of mass the local Catholic Church provides space for organizations, academics and community leaders to meet with immigrant churchgoers. As an immigrant woman, Lydia, explains,

> Community organizations come from as far as Raleigh to inform us of our rights. We are learning. They tell us that we have the right to a lawyer, that we have the right to not sign something we don't want to sign, that we don't have to open the door for an immigration agent.

At a more personal and private level, religion is a place of refuge and comfort for Latino immigrants. Recognizing that they could be deported any time, immigrants more than ever turn to the church, their clergy and their faith not just for information but also for protection, guidance and strength. Jessica, a regular attendant of the Catholic Church in Johnston County, stated:

> I am always afraid. Because this is not my country I always feel like I am being pursued. I know it is your country and your laws and that we have to respect those laws, but I also know it is not right. Men made these borders and I know God did not make any borders. It is to God we turn during these hard times.

Immigrants increasingly feel they are being expelled or banished from their residences and community. As Javier comments, 'They have put a stop on our IDs. Without one, you can't rent a house, turn your power on, or get insurance to legally drive your car. When immigrants lose electricity, they often move in with others that have it.'

As in other Latino communities throughout the United States, some immigrants have responded to local policing and social exclusion by withdrawing from the community. Settled immigrants reported no longer attending community events or visiting the library and avoiding public places like parks. Immigrants without drivers' licenses explained that they spend most of their non-working hours in their homes because it is the safest way to avoid detection by the police. This means they no longer go out to eat at local restaurants nor do they frequent churches or stores with any kind of regularity. As a result, community policing has hit especially hard businesses that cater to Latino clients. Owners of these businesses report that their sales have plummeted between 30 and 90 per cent in the past two years, and they attribute most of this decline to the loss of Latino clientele. Restaurant managers and owners, in particular, complain that their sales have declined significantly because Latino customers fear apprehension if they drive locally.

Some immigrants have stopped investing in a long-term future in North Carolina and are instead preparing for the possibility of going home. Immigrants reported that they stopped shopping on a regular basis for clothes, furniture, cars and other expenditures that tie them to life in the United States. The more successful immigrants send most of their earnings to family members in their home communities. This way, they reasoned, they will have savings waiting for them back home if they are deported. The less successful immigrants, in contrast, rely on money from home to tide them over until the economy picks up.

Others at risk of deportation are seeking dual citizenship for their children so that papers are in order should the family return home. As one immigrant woman explained, 'If I am deported and need to take my children home, without dual citizenship they will not be eligible for social services or an education.' Her worries are not isolated. The Mexican consulate in Raleigh, North Carolina, reports that, as a result of strict immigration laws and the growing Mexican population in the state, requests for dual citizenship have skyrocketed, from 416 applicants in 2005 to 4,918 in 2010 (Fox News Latino 2011).

Unable to overcome local enforcement operations and fearing apprehension, detention and family separation, some migrants have returned home. Community leaders estimated that 30 to 40 per cent of the undocumented immigrant population in the county have involuntarily returned to their homes in Central America and Mexico. These local trends in return migration are also suggested at state and national levels. In North Carolina, the undocumented population fell from 350,000 to 275,000 from 2007 to 2009. At the national level, the number fell to about 11.1 million in 2009, after peaking at 12 million in 2007 (Passel and Cohn 2010). The Mexican government confirms a reversal in migration trends. Not only are fewer Mexicans heading north because of the economic recession and stricter immigration laws, but almost a million returned home from 2007 through 2009 (Pinkerton 2009).

Some returns are voluntary, temporary and planned, while others are forced, permanent and unplanned. This distinction has important implications for family relationships and reintegration opportunities. Migrants who voluntarily return home have made the necessary preparations to ease integration. As forced returners, deportees may experience the loss of work, separation from family and multiple traumas as they attempt reintegration into a country they left years before. The contrasting stories of Roberto and Armando are instructive.

In the early 1990s, Roberto left his village in Guanajuato and headed north to Georgia, following the dream of many of his friends and family. Like most of his friends he started in the poultry business, but with time located an apprentice job in a furniture factory, eventually becoming a master carpenter. On one of his return trips to Mexico he fell in love and married. By 2008 he had achieved his migration goal. He packed up his new pickup truck with boxes of tools purchased in the United States and returned to Mexico to be with his wife and children and start a business. He enrolled in entrepreneurship classes to learn the ropes of starting a business in Mexico, and approached the president of a programme for return migrants, *Bienvenido Paisano*, about a loan. The president initially offered him a loan of 200,000 pesos to be paid back over six years but later reneged and cut the amount to 100,000 pesos with a one-year payback period. He decided against the loan. When one author (Hagan) interviewed Roberto in 2010, he had established a thriving carpentry business that specialized in the building and remodelling of US-style homes, for which there is a growing niche among return migrants. He had eight workers, all return migrants and trained carpenters. He credits his success to his skills, a US approach to business and a supportive family.

When Armando headed to California in 1980 he was a boy under 13 years of age. He made his way to the border where he was met by an uncle who guided him to his relatives in Redwood City, California. His first job was as a night dishwasher in a Mexican restaurant. He learned English watching MTV and at the age of 18 earned his GED and by age 24 had earned a certificate from an auto mechanic school. Within a decade, Armando was self-employed, had three workers and was bringing in $20,000 a month. His personal life was also a success – he had met and married Maria and they had four children. He was eligible for legal status under IRCA, but as he said, 'I just didn't think it was necessary'. All was fine until one day in 2008 when he was stopped for a traffic violation and deported to Tijuana. Armando tried to re-enter the United States but was apprehended and warned that he was now barred from re-entry for ten years.

After deciding to wait the ten years and attempt a legal re-entry through family reunification, Armando made his way to Oaxaca, where he had friends, but found that he lacked the skills to enter the auto mechanic industry. Unlike the United States where the industry relies on advanced technology and accessible new parts, in Mexico mechanics must learn to rebuild worn-out parts, skills that required Armando to return to night school. His excellent English skills landed Armando a job as a waiter in a tourist restaurant in Oaxaca. When Hagan interviewed him in 2010 he had not seen his children in five years and his wife had remarried. Despite his personal and financial setbacks since his removal from the United States, Armando counts himself lucky. His younger brother, Felix, who spoke little Spanish, was deported several years after Armando. He found himself in the wrong place at the wrong time and was killed by members of the drug cartel *La Familia* for witnessing a murder.

The lives of Armando and Felix and their US families were literally devastated both financially and emotionally through deportation. Roberto's family has been spared these costs because of his planned return. In neither case, however, has the Mexican government assisted in their reintegration, a response that was also reported by more than 94 per cent of the return migrants interviewed.

Implications for theory and policy

Our findings indicate that, although liberal democracies like the United States have historically undertaken expansionist phases of immigration (Freeman 1995), they will nonetheless embrace simultaneous restrictive measures in times of economic recession or of rising concerns for national security. Thus, the concept of 'the liberal democratic paradox' needs qualification. Faced with elevated goals of enforcement, such as in the Endgame mission, enforcement bureaucracies may develop a momentum that overtakes concern for the welfare of apprehended immigrants. In other words, the liberal democratic paradox is not fixed and constant, but a condition that shifts with overriding public sentiment and bureaucratic imperatives. Concern for the rights of migrants in the high offices of policy-making means little if not put into practice at the level of actual enforcement.

Our findings support the arguments of others that a host of political and bureaucratic actors and conditions explain variations in enforcement outcomes at the local level. In North Carolina, without a strong base of immigration-friendly voters and elected officials, Latino immigrants are powerless to lessen the impact of stepped-up enforcement strategies under the 287(g) programme. The criminalization of immigrants by local elected officials has fuelled anti-immigrant sentiment and justified local policy. Newcomers are increasingly blamed for crime in counties throughout the nation, although these arguments have been discredited by research that shows that crime rates have actually declined in counties where immigration has increased, suggesting that the presence of immigrants serves a protective function in neighbourhoods (Sampson, Morenoff and Raudenbush 2005).

The long- term implications of what Kanstroom (2007) terms post-entry social control are evident. The interior enforcement measures pursued by ICE raise the normal requirement that immigrants must be in the country legally almost to a litmus test of social control. It is no longer enough for immigrants to be in the country legally – they must now conform to unprecedented behavioural standards, even retroactively, or face what for many amounts to permanent banishment.

Our research also has policy implications for the United States and Mexico. Reported declines in the size of the undocumented population at local, state and national levels suggest that US enforcement operations may be effective in the short run, but at a significant cost to immigrant communities and families. Local enforcement initiatives like 287(g) have broken down trust between immigrants and police. Many deportees are long-term residents who are connected to the United States by culture, labour and, most importantly, kinship. Because deportation severs migrants from income-generating activities in the United States, it imposes economic costs on family members in the US household who then ironically may become dependent on government programmes for assistance in the absence of the breadwinner. Deportation also imposes enormous emotional and psychological traumas on families through temporary or permanent separation.

In the context of the increasing involuntary returns of their citizens, the Mexican and Salvadoran governments need to take seriously the problem of return migration. In recent years both governments have established various economic programmes for their citizens living abroad, including fund matching, micro-credit and other financial and administrative incentives. What are lacking are social and economic integration programmes that facilitate the well-being of their citizens returning home and tap into the skill sets they bring with them. Return migrants are extraordinary resources who, if supported properly, can help stimulate the Mexican and Salvadoran economies and create good jobs at home – all of which helps to reduce the push factors of migration.

References

ALEINKOFF, T. A., MARTIN, D. A. and MOTOMURA, H. 2001 *Immigration and Nationality Laws of the United States: Statutes, Regulations, and Forms*, St. Paul, MN: West Group

AMNESTY INTERNATIONAL USA 2009 *Jailed without Justice: Immigration Detention in the USA*, Washington, DC: Amnesty International USA

BADA, XOCHITL *et al.* 2010 *Context Matters: Latino Immigrant Civic Engagement in Nine U.S. Cities*, Washington, DC: Woodrow Wilson International Center for Scholars

BUFF, RACHEL IDA 2008 'The deportation terror', *American Quarterly*, vol. 60, no. 3, pp. 523–51

CAPPS, RANDY *et al.* 2007 *Paying the Price: The Impact of Immigration Raids on America's Children*, Washington, DC: Urban Institute

CAPPS, RANDY *et al.* 2011 *Delegation and Divergence: A Study of 287(g) State and Local Immigration Enforcement*, Washington, DC: Migration Policy Institute

CATHOLIC RELIEF SERVICES 2002 *Informacion al April 1999 – March 2002*, San Salvador: Programa de Atención a Los Immigrantes Salvadorenos, ¡Bienvenido a Casa!

ELLERMAN, ANTJE 2009 *States against Migrants: Deportation in Germany and the United States*, New York: Cambridge University Press

EL SALVADOR MINISTERIO DE JUSTICIA Y SEGURIDAD PUBLICA 2009 *Estadísticas de Migración*, San Salvador: Ministerio de Justicia y Seguridad Publica, http://www.seguridad.gob.sv/index.php?option=com_content&view=article&id=98&Itemid=172

FLORES, LISA 2003 'Constructing rhetorical borders: peons, illegal aliens, and competing narratives of immigration', *Critical Studies in Media Communications*, vol. 20, no. 4, pp. 362–87

FOX NEWS LATINO 2011 'More Mexicans are seeking dual citizenship for their children', http://latino.foxnews.com/latino/news/2011/02/15/mesicans

FREEMAN, GARY 1995 'Modes of immigration politics in liberal democratic states', *International Migration Review*, vol. 29, no. 4, pp. 881–903

GIBNEY, MATHEW J. and HANSEN, RANDALL 2003 *Deportation and the Liberal State: The Forcible Return of Asylum Seekers and Unlawful Migrants in Canada, Germany, and the United Kingdom*, Switzerland: United Nations High Commission for Refugees, Evaluation and Policy Analysis Unit

HAGAN, JACQUELINE 2008 *Migration Miracle: Faith, Hope and Meaning on the Undocumented Journey*, Cambridge, MA: Harvard University Press

HAGAN, J., ESCHBACH, K. and RODRIGUEZ, N. 2008 'U.S. deportation policy, family separation, and circular migration', *International Migration Review*, vol. 42, no. 1, pp. 64–88

HOFFMAN, ABRAHAM 1974 *Unwanted Mexican Americans in the Great Depression: Repatriation Pressures, 1929–1939*, Tucson, AZ: The University of Arizona Press

HUMAN RIGHTS WATCH 2009 *Forced Apart (By the Numbers): Non-Citizens Deported Mostly for Nonviolent Offenses*, New York: Human Rights Watch

KANSTROOM, DANIEL 2007 *Deportation Nation: Outsiders in American History*, Cambridge, MA: Harvard University Press

LYTLE HERNANDEZ, KELLEY 2006 'The crimes and consequences of illegal immigration: a cross-border examination of Operation Wetback, 1943–1954', *Western Historical Society*, vol. 3, no. 1, pp. 421–44

MENDOZA, MARCELA and OLIVAS, EDWARD M. 2009 'Advocating for control with compassion: the impact of raids and deportations on children and families', *Oregon Review of International Law*, vol. 11, no. 1, pp. 111–22

NGUYEN, MAI and GILL, HANNAH 2010 *The Costs and Consequences of Local Immigration Enforcement in North Carolina*, Chapel Hill, NC: Institute for the Study of the Americas

NIOLET, BENJAMIN 2008 'Sheriffs line up 3,100 to deport', *Raleigh News and Observer*, http://www.newsobserver.com/news/nation_world/story/94071.html

PASSEL, JEFFREY and COHN, D'VERA 2010 *U.S. Unauthorized Flows are Down Sharply since Mid-Decade*, Washington, DC: Pew Hispanic Center

PHILLIPS, S., HAGAN, J. and RODRIGUEZ, N. 2006 'Brutal borders: examining the treatment of deportees during arrest and detention', *Social Forces*, vol. 85, no. 1, pp. 93–110

PINKERTON, JAMES 2009 'Reversing course for survival', *Houston Chronicle*, http://www.chron.com/disp/story.mpl/special/immigration/6348003.html

RODRIGUEZ, N. and HAGAN, J. 2004 'Fractured families and communities; effects of immigration reform in Texas, Mexico and El Salvador', *Journal of Latino Studies*, vol. 2, no. 3, pp. 328–51

SALTER, M. B. 2004 'Passports, mobility, and security: how smart can the border be? *International Studies Perspectives*, vol. 5, no. 1, pp. 71–91

SAMPSON, R., MORENOFF, J. and RAUDENBUSH, S. 2005 'Social anatomy of racial and ethnic disparities in violence', *American Journal of Public Health*, vol. 95, no. 1, pp. 224–32

SOUTHERN POVERTY LAW CENTER 2009 *Under Siege: Life for Low-Income Latinos in the South*, Montgomery, AL: Southern Poverty Law Center

US CENSUS BUREAU 2010 *American Fact Finder*, Washington, DC: US Census Bureau

US DEPARTMENT OF HOMELAND SECURITY (DHS) 2003 *Endgame: Office of Detention and Removal Strategic Plan, 2003–2012, Detention and Removal Strategy for a Secure Homeland*, Washington, DC: US Immigration and Customs Enforcement (ICE)

——— 2006 *Treatment of Immigration Detention at Enforcement Facilities*, Washington, DC: US Department of Homeland Security. Office of the Inspector General

——— 2008 *2007 Yearbook of Immigration Statistics*, Washington, DC: Office of Immigration Statistics

——— 2009 *2008 Yearbook of Immigration Statistics*, Washington, DC: US Department of Homeland Security, Office of Immigration Statistics

——— 2010 *2009 Yearbook of Immigration Statistics*, Washington, DC: US Department of Homeland Security, Office of Immigration Statistics

US GOVERNMENT ACCOUNTING OFFICE 2009 *Immigration Enforcement: Better Controls Needed over Program Authorizing State and Local Enforcement of Federal Immigration Laws*, Washington, DC: Government Accountability Office

US IMMIGRATION AND CUSTOMS ENFORCEMENT 2009 *Delegation of Immigration Authority Section 287(g) Immigration and Nationality Act*, Washington, DC: US Immigration and Customs Enforcement

WEISSMAN, D., HEADEN, R. and LEWIS PARKER, K. 2009 *The Policies and Politics of Local Immigration Enforcement Laws*, Raleigh, NC: NC ACLU, Chapel Hill, NC/ Immigration and Human Rights Policy Clinic at the University of North Carolina at Chapel Hill

Turning refugees into 'illegal migrants': Afghan asylum seekers in Europe

Liza Schuster

Abstract

Each year refugees transit southern EU Member States where in theory they should claim asylum but where in reality they have little chance of being able to make a claim, and almost no chance of having it examined properly, much less being actually granted asylum. This paper argues that the current EU regime turns some refugees into undocumented migrants – 'illegal migrants' in political and public discourse – and shields EU Member States from their international legal obligations. The article illustrates the effect of EU asylum policy through a case study of a group of young Afghan men in Paris.

Introduction

By 2008, the European Union had in place a European Asylum policy regime and a legal framework based on an 'absolute right to seek asylum' and 'full and inclusive' application of the 1951 Convention relating to the Status of Refugees (Commission 1999, see also Vedsted-Hansen 2005). However, EU legislation and policy seems to be largely an exercise in evading responsibility. There have been a number of critiques of the regime on a variety of grounds (Vedsted-Hansen 2005, Schuster 2005, Spijkerboer 2007) but this article concentrates on one effect of the regime in particular – that is, the way in which the battle to combat 'abuses of the asylum system' turns some refugees into undocumented migrants, or 'illegal migrants' (see also Samers 2003). While accepting that not everyone who applies for asylum meets the definition contained in the 1951 Convention, I wish to stress here that it is not recognition that makes one a refugee, but the circumstances that caused one to flee. Throughout the sometimes very long process that leads to recognition (or refusal), someone forced to flee their country of habitual residence due to fear of or actual persecution does not cease to be a refugee, even though during and after that process one may be categorized as an asylum seeker, a failed asylum seeker or an 'illegal migrant'.[1] The critique of EU policy presented here relies on the experiences of Afghans in Paris.

For eighteen months from July 2008, the author volunteered on a twice weekly basis with the *Collectif de soutien des exilés du 10ème*, a small group of Parisians from different walks of life who visit the places where these Afghans gather to eat – usually Salvation Army food distribution points.[2] They provide information and answer questions on the European regime, seeking asylum in France (and other EU countries), their rights to accommodation, where to get medical treatment, French lessons, legal advice, and recognition rates across the EU. Working with this group has provided a sharp insight into how the European asylum system does and does not work for a group of people coming from a situation of generalized violence and individual persecution. By exploring the impact of Dublin II and Eurodac on a group of young men who do not behave in the manner expected (i.e., claim asylum in the first safe third country they enter) we seek to demonstrate that Dublin II and Eurodac cannot achieve their putative goals (of distributing the asylum 'burden' more equitably) but instead turn refugees into 'illegal migrants'.

The article is informed by direct conversations with young Afghan men at places where they gather (soup kitchens and parks), by Saturday afternoon meetings between them and volunteers, by observations, and by the summaries of the conversations which volunteers, including the author, posted online each evening. The choice of interlocutors was dictated by the profile of the Afghans in the tenth *arrondissement* who were almost exclusively young men, ranging in age from about thirteen to thirty. This population constantly changes as people arrive and depart, some after just a few days, others after many months. Some are returning to Paris, having been deported to another EU Member State following the discovery of their fingerprints in Eurodac. Some have been returned to France from the UK, and of these, some are determined to return to the UK (even some who have previously been deported from the UK to Afghanistan) because they have family there or because they know they will be able to find work there. Others want to try somewhere else. Still others are in the French asylum system awaiting a decision on their case. There are two other groups. The first has been refused asylum by the French government, so are 'rejected asylum seekers' but as France finds it difficult to deport to Afghanistan, they are stuck in France without status as 'illegal migrants'. The second group has applied for asylum but having been told that the French government is not obliged to examine their claim as their fingerprints have been found in Eurodac, knows that they face deportation to Greece, or Hungary, or another EU Member State. This group knows that if returned to those countries they have no chance of being recognized as refugees, and that they risk deportation from, for example, Greece to Turkey. It is this group that are trapped, knowing they cannot go back, but knowing also that they cannot go on. They are the primary concern of this paper.

Given the difficulties of obtaining informed consent under these circumstances, an early draft of this paper was translated into Dari and circulated to some of the Afghans for comment. The conversations took place with the author in Dari, Greek, French, English, and Italian. The two national cases explored (i.e., Greece and France) serve as case studies: Greece illustrates more generally the case of south-eastern EU Member States with low refugee recognition rates, while France is one of the north-western Member States with higher recognition rates. This group of young men is currently in France, and almost all have entered through Greece, which according to the Dublin Convention is where they should stay, and because the Dublin Convention serves to underline a distinction between countries of first entry, such as Greece, and countries presumed to be preferred destinations, such as France. While such a small study does not allow generalization, many of the experiences related here are common to all asylum seekers in the EU. In the final section, the author reflects on the consequences, intended or otherwise, of turning refugees into 'illegal migrants'.

Asylum law in the EU

The EU Member States have put in place a series of asylum directives to ensure a harmonization of policy across the EU so that all those applying for asylum in EU Member States are guaranteed certain basic conditions of reception and access to the asylum procedures, protections, and rights (see Schuster 2011). The intention is to reduce the incentives for those seeking asylum to move from state to state. The core principle of this European system, embodied in Dublin II (the revised version of the Dublin Convention 1997), is that whichever state allows someone to enter or remain in their territory is responsible for examining that person's application for asylum – *and that no other state need examine that claim*. There are a number of problems with the Convention: it places heavy burdens on countries of first arrival, such as Greece, Italy, and Spain (ECRE 2006); it allows the application of the safe third country concept (i.e., not the state of origin or the state in which the person wishes to make a claim, but the first safe country reached by the asylum seeker after leaving their country of origin or habitual residence), which permits Member States to expel asylum seekers to states outside of the EU [Art. 3 (5)], such as Turkey, from where people are *refouled* to states where their lives and liberty are in danger; and most seriously, by relieving all but one state of the duty to examine a claim, it turns refugees into 'Dublinized' asylum seekers, that is, those in limbo waiting to see whether and where their claim will be examined.[3]

Most of the literature on the decision making of asylum-seekers highlights their need to leave and the reliance of asylum seekers on smugglers who often make decisions on destinations (Robinson and Segrott 2002, Gilbert and Koser 2006). Others have pointed out that where asylum seekers (or their families) do plan where they are going, these decisions are based on factors such as family or social networks, language skills, or cultural affinity (often the result of colonial links), which are at least as important in the choice of where to apply (Boyd 1989, Gurak and Caces 1992, Koser 1997, Efionayi-Mäder et al. 2001). Nonetheless, the young men encountered in Paris, whose daily lives are rendered very difficult by the legal constraints, continue to exercise a considerable degree of agency. The differences that remain between EU Member States mean they moved around Europe trying to find some way into regularity and some assistance with accommodation and rebuilding their lives. It seems that once they arrive in Europe they adjust their plans as they learn about differences in recognition rates and in reception conditions, meet other people further along in the process, and see for themselves the treatment meted out by different EU states (see below). While in recent months, a small group of people have given up and agreed to return 'voluntarily' to Afghanistan, for some of the people encountered in Paris, deportation, whether to another EU state, to Turkey, Iran or even to Afghanistan itself, did not put an end to their journey. It had become just another hurdle to be overcome in the struggle to build a future. K had been returned five times from Turkey to Iran, each time spending about a month in prison, and twice from Greece to Turkey. He laughed: 'After the first time, when they pointed the Kalash at me and told me to lie on the ground, I just did as I was told. I got used to it. I knew I would get out and try again.' Five of the men met in Paris were making a second journey from Afghanistan, having already been through an asylum process in the UK, but having been deported back to Afghanistan (one had been deported to Afghanistan twice over a period of three years). The responses of these men to their treatment by EU Member States is a testament both to their determination and to the pressures that push them onwards. However, EU states punish those who try to exert some degree of control over where they make their claim by using the Dublin Convention and the Eurodac system to return them to other

Member States. Where this is not possible they place them in accelerated procedures or refuse to examine their claim at all, or simply leave them in limbo for as long as possible – if after six months trying the host state is unable to send someone back to a safe first country, they are obliged to take responsibility for the claim. However, it is not uncommon to find some, like K, who have had to wait eighteen months before responsibility for examining his claim was accepted.

The numbers of asylum applicants who are successfully removed to 'safe third countries' are very few. Between September 2003, when Dublin II came into effect and December 2005, approximately 11 per cent of the total number of applications made in the EU were examined under Dublin II, but due to fingerprints missing from Eurodac, a failure of Member States to issue travel documents, and the failure of some applicants to cooperate-only 2.8 per cent were actually returned – raising questions about cost and efficacy. Nonetheless, the 11 per cent of asylum applicants 'under Dublin' equalled 55,300 people – that is a large number of people in limbo (Cimade 2008, p. 36). In some cases, they become caught between states in a no-man's land outside the law.

Negotiating the European asylum regime: an illustration

Afghanistan is the fourth most important source country of asylum-seekers in the industrialized world (most, approximately five million, are in Iran and Pakistan). 18,500 asylum applications were submitted by Afghans in 2008 in *industrialized* countries, the highest since 2002 (29,400 claims), with most in the United Kingdom (3,700 claims), Turkey (2,600), Greece (2,300), and Italy (2,000). UNHCR attributes the increase in the number of Afghans arriving to the deteriorating security situation in Afghanistan (UNHCR 2008a), but according to many of the Afghans in Paris who have lived in Iran and Pakistan, the hardening of the governments' attitudes in those two countries also plays a role. France hosts relatively few Afghans, with the number of asylum applications increasing from 184 in 2007 to 249 in 2008 (UNHCR 2008)· The French Office for the Protection of Refugees and Stateless Persons (OFPRA) recorded a slightly higher number of Afghan applicants in 2008 (281) of whom 104 were granted either refugee status or subsidiary protection (OFPRA 2009). In Greece, none were granted asylum that year. In the table below, the second row of figures refers to the percentage of Afghan asylum applicants who are either recognized as (Convention) refugees or are given some form of subsidiary status. In most EU Member States, those Afghans allowed to make and pursue a claim have at least a 50 per cent chance of being granted some form of status, but the wide variety in recognition rates inevitably raises the question of what criteria are being used to assess claims.

The role of Greece in turning refugees into illegal migrants

Yunnan and *angusht* are words that crop up again and again in conversation with the Afghans in Paris. They are the Dari words for 'Greece' and for 'fingers'. Almost all the Afghans have come through Greece,[4] and many have had their fingerprints taken there. Once they come to the attention of the authorities anywhere else in the EU, if their fingerprints are found in the Eurodac database, it is to Greece that they will be returned – whether or not they have applied, or been allowed to apply, for asylum in Greece. Despite a sharp increase in the number of asylum applications in Greece from 12,267 in 2006 to 26,735 in 2007 (OFPRA 2008), and 38,000 by January 2009 (UNHCR 2009), these numbers are low compared to other Member States given that Greece is the first EU state reached by many potential asylum seekers, especially those coming from Afghanistan.

Asylum applications from Afghans are low in Greece both because the authorities make it very difficult for them to claim asylum, and because those who have tried to claim point out to newcomers that that they have no chance of recognition if they do apply. Over the course of the last two years, Afghans in Paris have described being arrested on crossing the border between the two countries and thrown in jail near Alexandropoli, near the Turkish border. F recounted how 'after twenty days, when there was about one hundred of us, Greek "commandos" came and made us go to the river (the Evros). They put ten of us in a boat and then went back for more'. On the Turkish side, they were forced off the boats at gunpoint. This is in sharp contrast to the claim made in response to a report from the Commission for Human Rights of the Council of Europe by the Greek authorities that:

> None of the asylum applicants are removed from our country, unless the relevant procedure is finalized, according to article 33, par. 1 of the Geneva Convention, article 3 of the EHRC and other international legal instruments. Additionally, after the finalization of the asylum procedure, no alien is transferred to a third country, where it is presumed that their lives or liberties are endangered (*non-refoulement* clause). (Hammarberg 2009)

Given these figures, there is clearly a strong disincentive to claim asylum in Greece, since making such a claim means one risks being rejected and deported to Turkey (though Greece does not deport to Afghanistan). Since the recognition rates are much higher elsewhere, clearly many who would be recognized as refugees in other countries are being turned into 'illegal migrants' in Greece, a status that follows them intermittently around Europe. However, although making a claim does not lead to recognition in Greece, nor does it automatically lead to rejection. In most cases, applicants are left without a decision, but not allowed to try for refugee status anywhere else. Dublin II means that having made a claim, unless one is a minor or travelling with children, no other EU Member State is obliged to examine the claim unless Greece in this case refuses to readmit the applicant.

It is not only the impossibility of being recognized as a refugee that causes people to move deeper into Europe, it is the daily experience of living without rights. Without a secure status, people are at the mercy of criminals and of the police. The Afghans in Paris tell of daily harassment by the Greek police: F had twice been run over by a police car, suffering a broken leg and a broken ankle; another had been picked up and put in cells three times in ten days; another aged fourteen had been kept in a cell for three days – imprisonment for three months is not uncommon. Two Afghans reported having spent three months in a prison near Alexandropoli without having once been allowed out of their cell – a cell they shared with thirteen others. Almost all told of physical beatings – some retaining the scars.

Nonetheless, the picture that emerges of the Afghans' experiences in Greece is not straightforwardly bleak. Many of the Afghans had found work in Greece, managed to save enough to continue their journey, and some had established warm relations with their employers, including one who said that he missed his employer who had treated him like a son. Others told of young Greek men and women who would visit the squatter camps in Patras and speak to them and try to assist in any way they could, one visiting a police station to argue for the release of an Afghan minor. Some have said they would have been happy to stay in Greece where they had work, learnt the language, experienced some integration, made some friends, but being 'illegal', having no papers, security, access to regular employment or welfare rights, no protection from arbitrary arrest, and harassment by police wore them down and encouraged them to move on in the search for recognition and a way out of 'illegality'.

Most of the Afghans seem to have mixed motives for moving on – negative experiences in Greece plus stories from contacts further afield, from contacts in other EU Member States that promise things will be better. A significant number know, or know of, members of their extended families or friends around Europe who have received papers and who are working, or who are working without papers. In some cases, they are expected and encouraged to come and join them. The port of Patras on the west coast of Greece was an important staging post for those heading to Italy, with between 2,000 and 3,000 Afghans camped in squalid squatters camps. In early summer 2009, these were again destroyed by the police in preparation for a concerted effort to reduce the numbers of undocumented migrants in Greece. Of those who try to make it across the Adriatic Sea, some are intercepted and returned to Greece. Others are found in Italy and if they can be identified – e.g., through Eurodac – as having transited Greece, will be returned there. Some of those in Paris say that they have been waved through – the Italian authorities have little desire to detain them. In the summer of 2009, I met two small groups of Afghans (four and five people) who had spent up to five years in Italy. All had either refugee status or subsidiary protection. They told me they had left Italy because they are frequently mistaken for Roma and as a result had experienced physical and verbal abuse. Their response to problems in Italy was to move on. As N explained in fluent Italian, 'why should I stay if they do not want me? How can I stay if I cannot work?', or in the words of another, 'papers don't matter there, the police still arrest me and beat me because I had no money to give them'. None I spoke to had thought to apply through legal channels for permission to change residence: 'Why should I ask – I want nothing, just work.'

Of course, it is not only negative experiences in first countries that cause people to continue their journeys. Among those who travelled through Greece or Italy were Z and M who had family members in Britain, and J who had friends in Switzerland. Dublin II allows for family reunion, but this is only for immediate family members and only for those who already have status as either a refugee or asylum applicant. Sometimes it is family members back home who dictate the destination. Others are drawn onwards by phone calls from friends, sometimes made on the journey. G told me that he was on a train in Italy, heading for Switzerland when a friend he hadn't seen for a year phoned him on his mobile and said he was in Paris, so he had changed his plans and come to join his friend. H, having spent three years in Greece and speaking good Greek, complained bitterly that what he had seen of France on Greek television and heard from his friends was a lie, that in France Afghans were treated worse than the small dogs cosseted by the Parisians, and that he couldn't wait to be deported back to Greece where he had already initiated a claim.

The role of France in turning refugees into illegal migrants

All of the young men over eighteen to whom I spoke, with the exception of three who had worked as translators for the French forces in Afghanistan, had had to go through the Dublin II process, regardless of the strength of their claim to refugee status. Before being able to apply for asylum in France, an applicant must request a temporary residence permit from the Prefecture. Immediately, before a claim is made, a search of the database will be made, and if a match is found, an application will be made to the Member State where the fingerprints were taken to return the person under the Dublin Regulation and they will not be issued the temporary (usually one month renewable) permit.[5] During this period of waiting, the individual is obliged to return regularly to the Prefecture. If the other state refuses the transfer request, the person is issued with a temporary permit and allowed to make an asylum claim. Of those Afghans who are allowed to make a claim, about 42 per cent will be granted some form of status (see Table 1). If the other state agrees to the transfer request, which only happens in the minority of cases, the applicant may be detained to await the issuance of the necessary *laissez-passez* and to facilitate the transfer. The disparity between recognition rates in Greece (0 per cent) and in France (42 per cent) means that returning people to Greece effectively turns some refugees into illegal migrants.

Afghans arriving in Paris for the first time are shocked by reception conditions of earlier arrivals in Paris. In response to a question about staying in France, C pointed to the others gathered around a fire under the Pont Jean Jaurès and said 'my friends have been here for months – I did not come for that'. France's inhospitality to Afghans is evident to new arrivals, who are shocked and disheartened to find friends and fellow Afghans sleeping in parks, under canal bridges, and on the streets, suffering from lice and scabies, or accommodated with alcoholics and drug addicts in the bedlam of emergency hostels. The winter of 2008–9 saw temperatures drop to -10C, to which the City of Paris' response was the provision for minors of twenty five beds in a hall. Each night there were approximately sixty Afghans, many without blankets or sleeping bags, trying to sleep along the canal St-Martin. On three or four occasions, I met exhausted young men who had walked all night, afraid that the cold would kill them if they lay down. Those left outside included some who had applied for asylum, so that L, for example, asked 'what's the point of trying to stay in France?'. Some decide to travel on and ask for asylum elsewhere. However, it is not just the lack of accommodation that pushes people to try elsewhere. Among the other push factors are the lack of training

Table 1. *Recognition rates (%) of Afghan asylum seekers in selected EU Member States*

	Aus.	Den.	Fin.	Fra.	Ger.	Gre.	Ita.	UK
Refugee status	44	4	0	36	29	0	12	8
Total positive decisions (ref status + subsidiary protection)	80	50	95	42	60	0	67	55

Source: Adapted from UNHCR (2009)

opportunities, the lack of work permits, and a growing anger and bitterness at their treatment. Some decide within days to continue their journey, unable to believe that they would be not be allowed to ask for asylum in other EU Member States, but others are forced to wait sometimes for months either because they have no money to continue their journey, or because they have been picked up and finger-printed by the French police so that should they make it to England, Demark, Finland, Norway, or Sweden, they would be returned to France.

The complexity of European asylum regimes leads to a profound lack of comprehension among most of the Afghans about how the system works – even when they have already been through that system, something that chimes with the findings of Gilbert and Koser (2006). The different documents people are given are rarely – contrary to European guidelines – translated into a language they understand. Even where the documents have been translated into Farsi (closely related to the Dari of Afghanistan), some, like K, are not literate in Dari or Farsi. It was common to have people pull out official documents from their transparent plastic folders and ask, not just for a translation, but for an explanation about what the document meant for them and advice as to what they should do. Support organizations in all EU Member States, like the *Collectif* in Paris, are overstretched and few have the language skills to explain to Afghans what the different pieces of paper, and/or the terminology used, mean. The language difficulties are inevitably compounded by the strangeness of this system and the difficulties in orientating oneself.

The reports of the *Collectif* each evening almost invariably record 'the usual questions about fingerprints'. The author has met six different Afghan men who, having applied for asylum in the UK and been rejected, were in Paris having returned from Afghanistan, trying to decide where to go next, unable to believe that their fingerprints would follow them wherever they go in Europe. On being told that on applying in France, they will be placed 'under Dublin' because they have fingerprints in Eurodac, the same person asks 'what if I go to Austria? Or Sweden? Or Spain?'. About three months after I last saw him, M arrived at the soup kitchen. He told me he had made it to London, but had been picked up almost immediately by the police and deported to Hungary. I asked him what his plans were and he told me that he would now try to get papers in France. When I said that the French authorities would probably also find his fingerprints in Eurodac, his companion said 'that's okay – you only get deported once. After that they let you stay'. On being told that some people had been deported two or three times, including to Afghanistan, they looked shocked but then recovered to say 'we will keep trying. What choice do we have? Don't worry – we will do something'. R, still waiting for a decision after two years in France, told me that if he was rejected he would go to England. Surprised, I said 'but you've made a claim here – you'll just be returned to France', to which he responded 'I'll change my name'. When I asked, what about your fingerprints, he smiled 'they took my fingerprints in Greece and in Italy, but the police here didn't find them, so maybe I will be lucky again'. A recurring question is why, if one country does not want them, they cannot travel to another to seek asylum.

Dublin II contains a humanitarian clause allowing Member States to choose to take responsibility for claimants with extended family in France, or in the event of illness, etc. In other words, France could decide to process the claims of those known to have passed through Greece on the grounds that contrary to the assumptions of the Dublin Convention, Afghan refugees will not be recognized as such in Greece, and risk being *refouled* to Turkey and beyond. Norway took that decision in 2008 and stopped returning Afghans to Greece in recognition of the likelihood that refugees would suffer, an action for which it was commended by Amnesty International (2008).[6]

In Afghanistan, many of these young men have worked and contributed to their families from their early years. Even the youngest has made an exhausting journey, demanding high levels of resilience and resourcefulness. They are used to having a role, to taking responsibility for themselves and their families, rather than having to wait to be told what to do by a state. K had left Afghanistan for Iran aged ten, with his three older brothers, and had started work in a factory aged eleven. Aged twenty four, A had already been economically active for ten years, working in a restaurant. Some tell of families waiting for financial help. M, already four years on the road, explained sadly that he had given up phoning his mother and sister who were living in Iran because he couldn't bear them crying and asking when he was going to help them. Writing on young refugee men in Nairobi, Jaji considers the implications 'of exile on the men's quest to live up to identities, responsibilities and statuses assigned to men in African contexts' (2009, p. 177, see also Ahmed 2009 on Pakistan). While there are clear differences between the largely Christian young men in Nairobi, exile represents similar challenges to Afghan asylum seeking men in Europe. Among the Afghans are traders, teachers, students, soldiers, welders, tailors, mechanics, labourers, farmers, and chefs. All are desperate to work and/or study. Like asylum seekers all across Europe from whatever nationality and of whatever gender, all the young men spoken to resented this period of enforced idleness, their dependence on handouts, and being grouped together with those who cannot fend for themselves.[7]

For some, this attack on their pride, their self-esteem, and qualities they have been taught to value, such as working hard and looking after one's family, is also an attack on their masculinity and leads to depression and psychological damage (see Jaji 2009). During the last eighteen months, there have been incidences of self-harm and threats of, and attempts at, suicide which have necessitated interventions by psychologists from *Médécins Sans Frontiers.* In Paris, they have no place, no purpose. They may still be needed at 'home' (though life there is continuing without them), but here in Europe they are treated as a burden, something that, once it can no longer be ignored, should be disposed of as quickly as possible (Bauman 2004).

Conclusion – taking and not taking responsibility

Every year hundreds of thousands of migrants, including refugees, from around the world, enter the Member States of the European Union. Many – perhaps the majority – will succeed and will build lives and families. They come looking for work, but also freedom of various kinds, rights, and security. The Member States of the EU are engaged in a struggle to evade responsibility for those seeking asylum, though some are prepared to go to harsher lengths than others. Those Member States who are the primary first entry points, such as Greece, carry a particularly heavy responsibility, one that for a variety of reasons they are clearly failing to meet. Some Member States recognize this and do not return children or families to Greece, but Dublin II allows Member States that are not first entry states, such as France, to evade responsibility for young men who are left in limbo. Eurodac and the Dublin Convention combined mean that a number of those Afghans in Paris stand little or no chance of making a claim and being accepted anywhere in Europe. This does not mean that they will be returned to Greece – in fact only a small number are – but that their chances of making a claim for asylum in France (or Britain, or Germany, or Austria) are limited. Less than half of these will be granted refugee or humanitarian status (OFPRA 2009) but very few will be returned to Afghanistan. Instead, they will swell the ranks of the *Sans Papiers,* the undocumented, the so-called 'illegal migrants'.

On the other hand, EU Member States expect them to cross the external borders of the EU furnished with authoritative documentary evidence of their ages, of where they have lived, of the persecutions that they have suffered, to make themselves known to the authorities, to wait patiently, surviving without recourse to public funds, without being visible, to accept whatever decision is made about their future, and to go where they are told, including back to Afghanistan. They are emphatically not expected to make choices or decisions, but instead to present themselves as passive victims, grateful for whatever minimal tolerance they are shown. These expectations are so far removed from the realities of these young men that they find them intolerable and unacceptable.

In an evaluation of Dublin II and Eurodac, the European Commission concluded that 'the Dublin Regulation is in general being applied in a satisfactory manner and that it does provide a workable system for determining responsibility for the examination of asylum applications', although the 'low rate of effected transfers of asylum seekers compared to accepted ones undermines considerably the effectiveness of the system' (2007). The report makes clear that Member States often transfer similar numbers between themselves, raising questions about the point of the system, especially in light of the damage caused to the individuals, whose interests were not considered.

Generally, the EU regime is inefficient in its own terms – it is costly, unwieldy, and doesn't achieve the goals for which it was designed. Many fail to gain the protection they need, not because they do not meet the criteria of the Geneva Convention, but because of systems like Dublin II and Eurodac, which allow states to delay the examination of claims for months and years, leaving thousands without legal protection. Nonetheless, tens of thousands of people are given refugee status every year (though relatively few given the numbers globally), but often only after long and damaging periods in limbo, and long, expensive, and wasteful procedures. Member States insist that asylum seekers cannot be allowed to choose where they make their claims and this would lead to unfair 'burdens' on some Member States. Aside from the hypocrisy of such claims emanating from Europe, which takes such a relatively small percentage of asylum seekers, currently the so-called asylum burden falls disproportionately on those Member States least well-equipped to cope – Greece, Cyprus, Malta, Spain, and Italy.

One is left with the distinct impression that EU Member States are engaged in a largely symbolic battle, with Dublin II and Eurodac symbolic weapons. However, the wounds inflicted on living, breathing human beings are all too real.

Acknowledgements

My sincere thanks to the anonymous reviewers, and to the editors Alice Bloch and Milena Chimienti for their helpful comments.

Notes

1. It would be just as possible and valid to write a paper about how the EU asylum system turns people in search of work into 'illegal migrants', 'bogus asylum seekers', and liars but that would be a different paper.
2. Although the volunteers refer to this group as the 'Exilés', they tend to refer to themselves as Afghans, so this is the term used here. Over eighteen months, I spent two

evenings a week at two or three locations where between 50 and 100 young Afghan men gather. With most, I conversed in English, French, or Greek, though we also used Italian and Dari. More on the work of the collective can be found at http://www.exiles10.org/. I was a member of the collective, but the other members knew that I am also an academic writing on migration.

3. UNHCR has regularly criticized Turkey's practice of deporting people to Iran and Iraq (see e.g., http://www.unhcr.org/4811e23c4.html).

4. This appears to be changing, as word of the difficulties in Greece spreads, and at the end of 2009 more and more young men in Paris had chosen to travel via Bulgaria and Serbia into Austria.

5. Since Dublin II originally conflicted with the French constitution, which guaranteed the right to claim asylum, the constitution was modified in 1993 (Bosquet 2006, p. 9).

6. However, in July 2008, this decision was partly reversed and Norway decided to resume returning adults to Greece, though on a case by case basis, and began to discuss tightening its procedures to deal with the increasing numbers. This decision was confirmed by the Norwegian Immigration Appeals Board on 7 May 2009 (IAB 2009). Grounds for the decision included the 'resourcefulness of the 'appellants', the decision of other Nordic countries to return, and the decision of the European Court of Human Rights, 'where it was decided that return to Greece in accordance with the Dublin II Regulation is not a violation of the European Convention of Human Rights, article 3'. These were held to outweigh the concerns voiced by UNHCR, by the European Council, and the IAB members themselves.

7. For most, the only accommodation available is in the emergency shelters, one of which, in Nanterre, is referred to as the *Camp-e-diwanna*, the madmen's camp. Even at the end of December, with temperatures below freezing, some preferred to sleep beneath the bridges of Paris rather than endure a night among alcoholics, drug users, and the mentally ill.

References

AHMAD, NABIL ALI 2008 'The romantic appeal of illegal immigration: gender, masculinity and human smuggling from Pakistan' in M. Schrover, J. Leun, L. Lucassen and C. Quispel (eds), *Illegal Migration and Gender in Global and Historical Perspective*, Amsterdam: IMISCOE/Amsterdam University Press, pp. 127–150

AMNESTY INTERNATIONAL 2008 *Amnesty International Report 2008: State of the World's Human Rights* [online], http://thereport.amnesty.org/eng/regions/europe-and-central-asia/greece [Accessed 14 May 2010]

BAUMAN, Z. 2004 *Wasted Lives: Modernity and its Outcasts*, Oxford: Blackwell

BOSQUET, E. 2006 'Le droit d'asile en France: politique et réalité', *New Issues in Refugee Research*, no. 138, Geneva: UNHCR

BOYD, M. 1989 'Family and personal networks in international migration: recent developments and new agendas', *International Migration Review*, vol. 23, no. 3, pp. 638–72

CIMADE 2008 *Le Gens du Dublin II*: Parcours juridiques de demandeurs d'asile soumis à une réadmission selon le règlement Dublin II, http://www.cimade.org/assets/0000/1266/dublin2.pdf [Accessed 14 May 2010]

COMMISSION DES COMMUNAUTES EUROPEENNES 1999 *Conseil Européen – Tampere: Conclusions de la Presidence* SI 1999/800, Brussels

ECRE 2006 *Report on the Application of the Dublin II Regulation in Europe*, Brussels: Europe Council on Refugees and Exiles, http://www.ecre.org/files/ECRE%20Dublin%20Report%2007.03.06%20-%20final.pdf [Accessed 14 May 2010]

EFIONAYI-MÄDER, D. *et al.* 2001 *Asyldestination Europa-Eine Geographie der ASYL-BEWEGUNGEN*, Zürich: Seismo

EUROPEAN COMMISSION 2007 'Report from the Commission to the European Parliament and the Council on the evaluation of the Dublin system [SEC(2007) 742]', http://eur-lex.europa.eu/LexUriServ/LexUriServ.do?uri = CELEX:52007DC0299:EN:NOT [Accessed 15 May 2010]

GILBERT, A. and KOSER, K. 2006 'Coming to the UK: what do asylum seekers know about the UK before arrival?', *Journal of Ethnic and Migration Studies*, vol. 32, no. 7, pp. 1209–25

GURAK, D. T. and CACES, F. 1992 'Migration networks and the shaping of migration systems', in Kritz, Lim and Zlotnik (eds), *International Migration Systems: a Global Approach*, Oxford: Clarendon Press

HAMMARBERG, T. 2009 'Report of the Human Rights Commission of the Council of Europe into the human rights of asylum seekers in Greece', http://www.statewatch.org/news/2009/feb/coe-chr-greece-report.pdf [Accessed 15 May 2010]

HUMAN RIGHTS WATCH 2008 'Stuck in a revolving door: Iraqis and other asylum seekers and migrants at the Greece/Turkey entrance to the European Union', http://www.hrw.org/sites/default/files/reports/greeceturkey1108web_0.pdf [Accessed 15 May 2010]

IAB 2009 'Conditional returns to Greece', press release May 7 2009, Norwegian Immigration Appeals Board, http://feed.ne.cision.com/wpyfs/00/00/00/00/00/0E/CA/2C/wkr0003.pdf [Accessed 15 May 2010]

JAJI, R. 2009 'Masculinity on unstable ground: young refugee men in Nairobi, Kenya', *Journal of Refugee Studies*, vol. 22, no. 2, pp. 177–94

KOSER, K. 1997 'Social networks and the asylum cycle: the case of Iranians in the Netherlands', *International Migration Review*, vol. 31, no. 3, pp. 591–611

OFPRA 2008 *Rapport 2007*, Paris: Office Français de Protection des Réfugiés et Apatrides, http://www.ofpra.gouv.fr/documents/Rapport_OFPRA_2007_BD.pdf

OFPRA 2009 *Rapport d'Activité*, Paris: Office Français des Protection des Réfugiés et Apatrides, http://www.ofpra.gouv.fr/documents/Rapport_OFPRA_2008_BD.pdf [Accessed 15 May 2010]

ROBINSON, V. and SEGROTT, J. 2002 'Understanding the decision-making of asylum-seekers', Home Office Research Series Paper 243, http://www.homeoffice.gov.uk/rds/pdfs2/hors243.pdf [Accessed 15 May 2010]

SAMERS, M. 2003 'Emerging geopolitics of illegal immigration in the European Union', *European Journal of Migration and Law*, vol. 6, no. 1, pp. 27–45

SCHUSTER, L. 2000 'A comparison of asylum policy in seven European states ', *Journal of Refugee Studies*, special issue, vol. 13, no. 1, pp. 118–32

SCHUSTER, L. 2005 'A sledgehammer to crack a nut: deportation, detention and dispersal in Europe', *Social Policy and Administration*, vol. 39, no. 6, pp. 606–21

SCHUSTER, L. 2011 (forthcoming) 'Dublin II and Eurodac: examining the (un)intended(?) consequences', *Gender, Place and Culture*

SPIJKERBOER, T. 2007 'The human costs of border control', *European Journal of Migration and Law*, vol. 9, no. 2, pp. 127–139

UNHCR 2008a 'UNHCR statement on subsidiary protection under the EC Qualification Directive for people threatened by indiscriminate violence', January, http://UNHCR_Statement_on_Article_15(c)_QD[1].pdf

UNHCR 2008b 'UNHCR position on the return of asylum seekers to Greece under the "Dublin Regulation"', http://www.unhcr.org/refworld/docid/4805bde42.html [Accessed 10 May 2010]

UNHCR 2009 *2008 Global Trends: Refugees, Asylum-seekers, Returnees, Internally Displaced and Stateless Persons*, Geneva: UNHCR (see Excel data sheets)

VEDSTED-HANSEN, J. 2005 'Common EU Standards on asylum – optional harmonisation and exclusive procedures', *European Journal of Migration and Law*, vol. 7, no. 4, pp. 369–76

Index

Page numbers in Italics represent tables.
Page numbers in Bold represent figures.